Contents

Nebraska,
Where Dreams Grow

To Tom

©1980, 1981, Miller & Paine, Inc.
All rights reserved
Printed in the United States of America
Library of Congress Catalog Number 80-84238

J & L Lee Company
Lincoln, NE 68505

ISBN 0-934904-15-4

Picture Credits

History of Nebraska 1881: pp. 1, 3. Nebraska State Historical Society (general collection and Solomon D. Butcher collection): pp. 5, 7, 11, 13, 15, 17, 22, 25, 31, 37, 40, 43, 49, 52, 55, 58, 61, 64, 67, 73, 76, 79, 82, 85, 88, 91, 94, 97, 100, 103, 106, 109, 112, 115, 118, 121, 124, 127, 130, 133. American Historical Society of the Germans from Russia: p. 19. Stuhr Museum of the Prairie Pioneer: p. 28. University of Nebraska Lincoln Archives: p. 34. Miller & Paine,: pp. 46, 142. Lebanon Daily Record, Missouri: p. 70. Lincoln Journal/ Star Printing Co.: p. 136, KOLN-TV, Lincoln: p. 139.
Cover photos from the Nebraska State Historical Society. (C898-F-3, S679-K-2)

Printed by Service Press, Henderson, NE 68371

BOHANAN BROS.' LIVERY AND EXCHANGE STABLE

Lincoln in 1880

Curious, isn't it, that even in her most booming years a century ago, Lincoln was genteel. Ebullient, brash, full of optimism, but -- well, respectable, full of middle-class respectability. In the fast-moving, pellmell rush to settle the Nebraska prairies a hundred years ago, Lincoln somehow escaped the wild, un-disciplined boom-town splash that marked many another Nebraska community in its formative years.

In September, 1880, when young J. E. Miller became a partner in the store that was to bear his name, the town was only a dozen years old and already had thirteen thousand inhabitants, the capitol, the university, the penitentiary and the insane asylum. It had progressed mightily from the tiny settlement along Salt Creek that had been named the state capital twelve years earlier.

Most of the buildings were still the box-like one-story affairs that had been hastily hammered together of raw lumber, some of them with tall false-fronts to give an aura of importance, but they were beginning to be replaced by substantial stone structures. The town was losing its wariness that the capitol might be taken from it -- after all, it had been here now for twelve years -- and 1879 had been a great year for newcomers.

1

The Lincoln telephone exchange had more than a hundred instruments in service; the gas light company had almost ten miles of mains; and Mayor John B. Wright and the council were considering a water works for the town. The post office had ten mails a day coming into the new four-story modern Gothic building built of gray sandstone from the Gwyer quarries on the Platte; the fire department at P and 10th had two steam engines (one named P.C. Quick after the volunteer chief); and the trains of the B and M railroad connected with the east and were chugging toward the west on the newly-established lines of the southerly route. The *State Journal,* one of three newspapers, employed eighty hands, many of them setting type for job printing. One of the three hotels, the Commercial, advertised itself as ''the greatest health resort west of Long Beach, celebrated mineral water spring . . . unsurpassed in America.''

There were three banks, four marble works, a pottery factory and a carriage-maker, lumber yards and hardware stores, wall paper and furniture dealers, grocery stores and druggists -- clearly, the town was here to stay. There was a cigar factory, and the Antelope brewery, west of town, bragged of its output of three thousand barrels of beer per year. Chamber of Commerce-type brochures did not mention the scores of saloons sprinkled throughout the business section, nor the gambling establishments and sporting houses that were as much a part of Lincoln as they were of every other raw young prairie village.

Other than its state institutions, however, what distinguished Lincoln from other, similar communities in the expanding Great Plains area was the range of its cultural activities. The town library, on the south side of O between 11th and 12th, was supported by a ¾ mill levy from the town; the five-year-old Harmonic Society had an orchestra as well as dramatic and singing groups, and the Lincoln Philharmonic had just been organized. The Capital City Cornet Band and Orchestra had started the year before. There were lodges -- four Masonic orders meeting in the ''elegant and commodious hall on the corner of O and 10th, over the First National Bank;'' the Knights of Honor; Royal Arcanum; and the Knights of Pythias, as well as the newly-organized Grand Army of the Republic post for Civil War veterans.

And there were churches, twelve of them including two small ones for colored congregations. And five temperance societies, the Red Ribbon one boasting two thousand members. Clearly, the town of Lincoln in 1880 was one of substance and stability.

STATE CAPITOL

How Lincoln Became the Capital

If it hadn't been for a last-ditch, desperate attempt by Omahans to keep the state capital in their town, you might be living in Capital City, or Douglas, rather than Lincoln. The story of how the capital came to be located in Lancaster county, rather than in Omaha, and how it came to be called Lincoln, is a long one involving squabbling politicians fighting with each other in the legislature. Politics were rough-and-ready in the old days. And the location of the capital was a significant plum.

When Nebraska became a territory in 1854, the only settlement was at Bellevue, a fur-trading post where missionaries had established a school for Indian youngsters. It was there that the first governor of the state, Francis Burt, came, but within two days of his inauguration, he died. His successor, Thomas B. Cuming, established the brash new Omaha City as his capital, the first legislature meeting on January 16, 1855, in a building on 9th street between Farnam and Douglas provided by the Council Bluffs and Nebraska Ferry Company.

3

There the state government functioned, in the only brick building in town, while representatives of other towns -- Bellevue, Nebraska City and others south of the Platte -- fumed and tried to get the seat of government moved. In January, 1857, the legislature passed a bill asking for another location, a town in Lancaster county to be called Douglas after Stephen A. Douglas, who had been instrumental in getting the Kansas-Nebraska Bill passed in Congress and the territory established. But then-governor Mark Izard vetoed the bill because a new capitol building in Omaha was already in the process of construction. In 1858, the legislature moved into the new building but there was so much dissension within the body that at one point, some of the senators scuffled and swung at each other and the dissidents seceded to meet in Florence. That fight eventually was settled, and the legislature resumed its sessions in the new capital in Omaha.

When Nebraska became a state in 1867, the Omaha partisans assumed that their town would continue to be the capital. After all, they had the building.

Not so, the people south of the Platte cried! They united to insist that a commission be appointed to locate the seat of government on a section of land between Seward, Saunders, Butler and Lancaster counties. This time the new city was to be called Capital City.

In an attempt to discourage the Democrats from south of the Platte, an Omaha senator said, ''All right, then, let's call it Lincoln!'' knowing how the Democrats still hated the name of that Republican President. But the South Platters were so adamant about wanting the capital that not even that suggestion stopped them -- and the town that was eventually established was called Lincoln.

Rather than following their instructions about location, however, the commissioners decided that the village of Lancaster on the banks of Salt Creek was the best site for the state government. Omaha didn't give up easily; its partisans said that ''with no river, no railroad, no steam wagon, nothing,'' ''nobody will ever go to Lincoln who does not go to the legislature, the lunatic asylum, the penitentiary, or some of the state institutions.''

To make sure the legislature didn't change its mind, the commissioners hustled to get the capital building up. Only one architect, only one construction company, answered their advertisements; only in a quarry near Beatrice could they find enough limestone for the building. They hired all the teams they could find to haul the stone to the site, and by December 1, 1868, the building was finished. It had cost $75,000; only $40,000 had been appropriated. And it was so poorly built that it started to fall down almost before the first legislature met there -- before long, it had to be replaced. But it was up -- and Lincoln was the state capital!

NUMBER 17

When the First Train Came to Lincoln

With the hot mid-summer sun pouring down through the wilting cottonwood leaves and heating the blue-clad passengers below, the first train chugged into the outskirts of Lincoln on the Fourth of July, 1870, marking the beginning of an era. For with railroad service assured, the capital city was no longer isolated from the rest of the world.

That first train was not an imposing sight. Its tall-stacked locomotive was probably standard gear, but its cars were not. The B and M didn't have passenger cars in the state yet -- they had to be ferried across the river at Plattsmouth -- and these were simply flat-cars with uprights in the corners to which slats were nailed to form a temporary roof. Over the slats were laid freshly-cut cottonwood branches as protection against wind and sun. Sitting upright in the benches, the passengers braved soot and cinders to ride fifty miles, all the way from Plattsmouth to the end of the track, seven miles east of Lincoln, on the first passenger service of the Burlington and Missouri River railroad in Nebraska.

The occasion, short on comfort but long on promise, celebrated the completion of the first fifty miles of the track that would, within three years, reach Kearny Junction to join the Union Pacific tracks.

5

For days, newspapers had heralded an excursion for the public, but the Fourth of July one, which seems to have been the first passenger junket, was a special one, a reunion of Civil War veterans in the first state meeting ever held in the raw new capital city. Fifty of the Boys in Blue, as men of the Grand Army of the Republic were called, boarded the train in Plattsmouth at 11 a.m., and perhaps others joined at way-stations; they arrived at Stevens Creek at 2:30 and disembarked to wagons and carriages which took them on into Lincoln. At 5 p.m., four hundred persons joined the procession which formed in Market Square, and with the Silver Cornet band leading the way, they marched on the capitol. Governor David Butler and other state and city officials followed in carriages, and at the end of the procession unidentified persons carried banners. General Silas A. Strickland was marshal of the day.

The ceremony at the capitol must have been interminable, with speeches, recitations of lengthy poems, a fulsome rendition of the Declaration of Independence, and a long oration delivered by General Livingston, orator of the day, all interspersed with songs, shouts and much waving of flags. At some time during the day, the ladies, never further identified, served a meal to 400 persons in the "extreme heat," and the veterans elected officers for the state organization. The newspaper account in the July 7 Plattsmouth *Herald* described the occasion in grim detail emphasizing the GAR part of it and paying little heed to the significance of the railroad journey. Presumably the tired veterans, their blue uniforms moist with sweat, boarded the train to return to their homes late that night.

If anybody present that day stopped to recognize the importance of the first railroad passenger train to Lincoln, he certainly must have felt it was most appropriate that the occasion be shared by the GAR. The railroad provided a means whereby settlers could come into the area south of the Platte, and many of the first ones were Union veterans.

On July 26, regular passenger service was opened to the city of Lincoln, and by the end of the year, sixty miles of road west from Plattsmouth were in operation. The ties were of oak, the rails were heavy, 57-pound ones, and all but six miles of the line had masonry abutments. It was a well-built railroad. And it needed to be, for in the next several decades, it would bring tens of thousands of newcomers and their gear to settle in Nebraska.

Immigration Societies

A century ago in hundreds of little villages in Russia, Germany, Sweden, and the province of Bohemia, the glories of the far-off place called Nebraska were known, pictured perhaps larger than life-size. Nebraska was painted as the Promised Land, the place where almost everybody wanted to go. Some knew it as a place where a cousin or a neighbor had gone and prospered, become a land-owner, probably a millionaire.

Those who didn't know about it from relatives learned about Nebraska from posters. In all parts of northern Europe, agents of immigration societies handed out brochures, nailed up brightly-colored posters printed in the language of the country, and talked to anyone who would listen, offering suggestions and help to get to the land of milk and honey.

Most of the immigration societies were connected in one way or another with the railroads. In return for building rails across the country, Congress had granted the Union Pacific, later the Burlington, twenty sections of land for each mile of track they constructed, an amount of land that eventually added up to seven

7

million acres in Nebraska, fifteen percent of the total land in the state. To sell the land and to stimulate colonization which would provide markets for their services, the railroad organized immigration societies whose agents fanned out into even remote villages to encourage settlers to come to Nebraska. The Burlington, then known as the B and M, was one of the most aggressive in securing settlers, many of them to Lincoln and beyond in southern Nebraska.

The agents helped the farmers and laborers in Germany, Bohemia and Wales gather their belongings, sold them tickets to Lincoln, and helped them onto the ships in Liverpool, or Hamburg, or Göteborg; prices per person ranged from £11-11/ to £24-11/5 depending on whether they came steerage and coach, or cabin class and sleeper. For a large group, a whole colony of persons traveling together, an agent would sometimes come along on the ship; otherwise, the newcomers crossed the Atlantic alone and went through immigration at Castle Garden, later Ellis Island, in New York, before they met another representative of the immigration society.

Many states, Nebraska among them, and most railroad lines, hired "runners" to meet the newcomers as they reached Manhattan to steer them to their particular area of the country, many of them taking advantage of the frightened, non-English speaking immigrants. But the newcomers who had prepaid tickets to Lincoln usually ended up there, mostly because the Burlington runners saw to it that they did.

Coach-class immigrants carried their own luggage aboard special railroad cars, called Zulus, which had slatted benches for seating and sleeping, and stoves for heating and cooking; the immigrants provided their own bedding and did their own cooking during the four or five days it took to get to Lincoln.

There the railroad provided temporary quarters for them, an Emigrant House, where they could stay "a reasonable length of time," free of charge, while they decided what tract of land they wanted to buy. The 24 x 100 foot wooden building included a kitchen and dining room with running water, enough sleeping quarters for ten families, and was located next to the depot so that passengers could be unloaded directly from trains. Later Emigrant Houses were established at Henderson and at Sutton to accomodate more westerly travelers. (The Union Pacific had no facilities.)

When the families finally separated at the Emigrant House to go to their own newly-bought lands, they knew that perhaps they would never see their compatriots again. But they were excited at the prospect of becoming Americans, and to many of them, that meant of course, millionaires.

The Blizzard of 1873

When the north winds howl and the sky turns white with blowing snow, old-timers spin yarns to youngsters about the blizzards of the old days. Since the two most famous ones, those of 1873 and 1888, are far in the past, who is to say that they weren't bigger and worse, after all?

The black-and-white blizzard of 1873, devastating because the homesteaders were completely unprepared for it, cut a 200 mile swath through central Nebraska, Platte, Sherman, Howard and Nance counties, south to the Kansas line and north beyond the South Dakota border.

Easter was late in 1873 -- April 13, to be exact -- and the day was warm and sunny. It had been such a mild, open winter that many farmers had plowed in February and by Easter had long-since had their seed in the ground. Trouble was, there really hadn't been much moisture. It had been a dry year.

About four o'clock that quiet Sunday afternoon, the air became deathly still, a frightening, oppressive calm. Clouds began to boil up in the northeast and black clouds rolled in from the southwest. With a roar, they seemed to collide,

9

dust and grit from the south driven with tremendous force by circling tornadic winds. The winds twisted buildings off their foundation, splintered boards, hurled furnishings and bedding for miles; the sand ground paint off homes, flailed the skin off the face and hands of a man who finally flopped to the ground and clung to tufts of grass to keep from being blown any further.

When the dust-storm passed, rain began to fall, temperatures dropped, and shortly the rain turned to sleet, then snow, and the wind came back. For four days and nights the snow fell and the wind blew, Tuesday night worst of all, piling snow higher than windows, beyond rooftops. Because many settlers in the area had not yet had time to build shelters and were still living in their covered wagons, they took refuge wherever they could. In one three-room cottage near Kenesaw, twenty-three people huddled together during the storm; near Inland, seven adults and four horses nervously sat out the storm in a half-built shanty while the horses gnawed away at the rough pine scantlings. Four people who took shelter in a low sod chicken-house found when they were rescued, four days later, that they could not stand up, they'd been hunkered down so long.

No one knows the number of people who perished. In Howard county, a mother and one daughter perished after they went for help when their roof collapsed. Because many of the people affected by the storm were transients or newly-arrived settlers, an accurate count of human loss could never be made. For months afterward, farmers found bloated bodies of horses and cattle which had frozen to death.

At no time did the temperature during the 1873 storm fall lower than 30 degrees, and the total amount of snow was not large -- in the draws, there was no snow at all -- but the drifting and the duration of the storm made it an awesome one.

LOG SCHOOLHOUSE IN SHERIDAN COUNTY

The Schoolchildren's Blizzard

The Blizzard of 1888 was far more catastrophic than the one of 1873 in terms of loss of human lives. Although it was of shorter duration -- eighteen hours rather than four days, it covered a larger geographic area -- the entire Great Plains area rather than central Nebraska, and thousands more settlers had moved into the area in the intervening fifteen years. Temperatures were much colder -- one old-timer claimed 58 degrees below, and the amount of snow which fell was tremendous.

The Blizzard of 1888 is known as the Schoolchildren's Blizzard because it started on Thursday afternoon as youngsters were leaving their country schools to walk across the prairie to their homes. Of the persons who perished in this raging storm, scores were children.

January 12 was such a warm day that some youngsters hadn't worn coats to school. Early in the afternoon the wind switched to the northeast and with a fury, the storm roared in, black clouds smothering the sun. The temperature plummeted, the winds accelerated, snow whitened the sky.

11

Many of the teachers, some no more than teen-agers themselves, were weatherwise enough to keep their students in the schoolhouse; they knew the perils of blizzards on the Plains. Those with a few strapping 17 or 18-year old students had help keeping the pot-bellied stove stocked, using desks, tables, whatever was available when the coal-bucket was empty, so that the youngsters would not freeze in the temperatures which had dropped to twenty degrees or more below zero through the night. Those children were rescued the next day, hungry but safe, by grateful parents, although one school board chastised a teacher who allowed the children to play cards as they huddled near the stove in the early-morning hours.

Youngsters who insisted on going home or who lived close-by the school were tied together, either with ropes or in one case with sleeve jackets so they would not become separated, and were allowed to return home. In Hastings, a blind man fought his way to the school and led a human chain of children to their homes near-by; he was not disoriented by the blinding snow.

When the wind blew off part of the roof of Minnie Freeman's school near Ord, she lined up the children and got them to safety to her rooming house a half-mile north. Another teacher, Lois May Royce, near Plainview, became lost as she took three children to her home two hundred rods north of the school. She took refuge next to a haystack but before daybreak three youngsters, huddled close to her for warmth, died. She lived but lost both feet and one hand was permanently disabled. A third teacher, Etta Shattuck in Holt County, was alone when she crawled into a haystack to get out of the storm, but although she was alive when she was rescued two days later she died after both frozen legs were amputated.

Many children did not make it home. Their frozen bodies were found a day or so later, some of them within hallo-ing distance of their homes.

Scores of reminiscences about the Blizzard of 1888 are recounted in the book *In All Its Fury,* compiled by W.H. O'Gara, edited by Ora A. Clement, and published by the Blizzard of January 12, 1888, Club. That book is dedicated to Pioneer Mothers, Fathers and Schoolteachers.

12

FIRST RESIDENCE IN LINCOLN WAS LUKE LAVENDER'S LOG CABIN AT 14 & O

Log Cabins and Dugouts

After Nebraska became a territory in 1854 and white men were allowed to settle here, the first settlers chose their homesteads in the wooded areas along the Missouri river, felling the cedar, oak and walnut trees for their log cabins. Later comers moved westward, selecting the rich lands along the streams that flowed west to east, building their homes from the ash, cottonwood and hackberries that grew along the riverbanks.

Although those stands of trees were never dense enough to be considered forests, still they provided building material for newcomers for the first dozen years after the state opened up to settlement. When the Union Pacific began felling trees in 1865 for railroad ties, eventually completely denuding the land for two hundred miles along the Missouri river, the new homesteaders had already gone farther west to seek land.

Along the Big Blue and the Nemaha to the south, the Elkhorn to the north, the Platte as far west as Grand Island, and in other areas where there was timber, the frontiersmen felled trees, notched logs, and built the same kinds of rough log cabins their forefathers before them had had in Indiana, Illinois, Pennsylvania, Kentucky. In time they set up saw-mills along the waterways and produced rough lumber from the wooded areas near-by.

Log cabins were the first homes in eastern Nebraska and in some other parts as well.

But before long, all the land along the streams was claimed, so that the next homesteaders had to be content with upland farms, the broad prairies where for miles there were no trees, not even along the little streams that flowed in the spring but were dry by summer. The qualities that made that land so attractive for farming -- no rocks to grub out before the plow could dig into the fertile soil, no trees to cut down and stumps to gouge out before the land could be planted -- also meant that there were none of the building materials that the newcomers had known in their former homes.

They had to use their ingenuity. They had to make do, a phrase that became a by-word on the prairie.

In ravines, in hillsides, the new settlers learned to dig into the bank and make dugouts, lateral caves dug out of the soil, with the roof overhead shored up with what timbers they could find. Since there was no way of providing windows for light or ventilation, and no door save the entrance, the dugouts were not large, seldom more than one room in size, but tall enough for a man to stand up and large enough for comfort. With blankets or buffalo robes across the entrance to protect against rain and snow and wind, dugouts provided shelter, families living in them cozily sometimes for several years before they could move into more sophisticated quarters.

Sometimes the crust of soil that formed the roof was so flimsy or so weakened by equinoctial rains that it gave way under stress. A few early-day stories from Custer County tell of startled homesteaders in their dugouts being awakened from a sound sleep to find that an animal or a horse-and-rider had crashed through the roof while racing across the prairie. Sometimes the dugouts, which ideally faced east, were so well-hidden that they were hard to find. A story from Exeter tells of a man who wandered around all night long on the prairie trying to locate his dugout in the starless night. When dawn came, he found he was almost standing on it.

Dugouts served purposes other than homes, for in Furnas county, the first jail was a dugout on the banks of Beaver Creek. In other cases, the dugout which served first as a home for settlers later was put to use as a storage cave after the family built a more permanent home.

The numbers of homesteaders who lived in dugouts were not as large as those who lived in log cabins or sod houses, but this form of housing was nonetheless significant in the early years of settlement in Nebraska.

14

THE RAWDING FAMILY SODDIE IN CUSTER COUNTY

Sod Houses

Out in the treeless plains of central and western Nebraska, homesteaders could not find the building materials they had known back home -- trees and rocks. All they had was the ground they stood on, soil bound together with heavy growth and the intricate root system of native wild grasses. The plainsmen of Nebraska, as well as those of Kansas and the Dakotas, borrowed ideas from the lodge-dwelling Pawnee and Mandan Indians, and created their houses of sod. They jokingly called it Nebraska marble.

They sought out a lagoon or damp area where the grass was thick and the roots wirey, and then with a special plow, called a grasshopper, they plowed strips a foot wide and cut them into two-foot blocks. Old-timers say that when they stabbed into the soil to make the first cut into the tough virgin sod, the soil gave a sort of sigh, as though it knew the old days were gone forever.

They slid the damp blocks onto a skid or platform and hauled it to the building site where the dimensions of the house had been marked with pegs and string and the ground cleared of grass. Sometimes the site had been laid out at night with stars as reference points.

Sod Houses

The blocks were laid up like giant bricks, without mortar, the moist blocks nestling together and settling to form a close, tight wall. Openings were left for windows and doors and later framed in, with oiled paper for the windows if no glass were available. The roof could be either flat or peaked to a center ridge-pole; it was made of timbers or brush covered over with sod. Eventually the sod dried to a hard, adobe-like consistency. Sod-house building became an art and some builders specialized in it.

The thick walls of the soddie insulated the house, making it cool in summer, warm in winter. But they also made the rooms dark, so dark, in fact, that people who went out-of-doors from a soddie always squinted at the bright light outside. Sometimes people in sodhouses calcimined the walls to make them light-colored, sometimes even papered the walls, which were so sturdy that the owners could pound nails in them to put up shelves for dishes and supplies. Frontier wives put bright potted plants on the wide window-ledges for bright spots of color in the small, usually two-room houses. And there were flowers on the roof, for the wild flowers that grew in the lagoon kept on blooming on the sod roof; Mark Twain, seeing a sodhouse near North Platte, remarked that it was the first time he'd ever seen a man's front yard on top of his house!

The tamped dirt floor was muddy after a rain. Unless the walls were carefully chinked, mice and other small field animals in the soil came along with the sod-blocks, and skittered inside the house. Early-day stories tell of pioneer mothers occasionally spotting a snake dangling from the ceiling, hanging over the crib of a sleeping child. And somehow, there always seemed to be bed-bugs associated with soddies.

Since soddies were low and hugged the ground, they were not flattened by windstorms nor lifted up by tornadoes. Insurance rates -- for sodhouses were sometimes insured -- were far less than those for frame houses, which blew off their foundations and were prey to fire, especially prairie fires which swept across the plains.

In time, other buildings were also made of sod -- barns, chicken houses, even an occasional fence, although a sod fence took up much space and wasn't really worth the effort. A large soddie, 18 x 36, in Holt county served as a sort of hotel for twenty people for a year; it was jocularly called The Grand Hotel. A number of early-day schoolhouses were also made of sod.

As soon as they could afford it, families who lived in soddies built more sophisticated homes of frame and moved into them, proud of their new status. But the great-great-grandchildren of some of those early-day sodhouse dwellers are now building sod-and-solar houses themselves, realizing that the insulation qualities of Nebraska marble make soddies as practical in an energy-saving world as they were a hundred years ago.

16

WILLIAM A. KRUEGER, JR. WITH HIS ICE HARVESTER ON SALT CREEK

The Ice Harvest

A century ago, when the cold winds of winter blew, Nebraska farmers bundled up in heavy garments and set out for the winter harvest: ice from near-by streams or ponds. Whereas other harvests in midsummer or fall were of growing things, to eat during the winter, this harvest was for use during the heat of the year, to keep food from spoiling.

In the late fall, some farmers began to prepare for the ice harvest by damming up a creek that flowed through their land, scraping and tamping enough dirt across the waterway that by the time of the first frost, a respectable little pond was ready. Others depended upon a nearby stream. Weeks later, after a period of intense cold, the crop was ready for harvesting, the ice frozen solid to a depth of eighteen inches or so.

Ice-harvesting was usually a family affair, as were most farming activities. On a clear, cold day in January, father and sons would bundle up in heavy winter clothing, as waterproof as possible, and load their implements into the spring wagon, hitch up the team, and drive to the pond. The day was a bright, clear one, neither too cold for comfort nor warm enough for any melting to take place.

17

With chalk or string or some other means of marking, the farmer marked off long straight lines on the pond and then intersecting ones to indicate the 20-inch squares that would be carved from the solid mass of ice. Then with an axe, he hacked at one spot, establishing a pivot point from which his sons would begin to saw. They could use any heavy rip-saws, for ice saws easily, but some families kept long-bladed, two-handled ones for their ice-harvesting, two boys at a time making short work of the job at hand. With rhythmic motions, the sawyers worked their way through the ice to the sand bottom of the pond, or in streams, to the water which flowed underneath.

After they had cut long, straight parallel lines, the ice-harvesters made the intersecting cuts for the blocks. As the squares took shape, others in the ice crew lifted up the blocks, either with tongs or with mittened hands. The first piece out was the hardest; it had to be pried and jimmied before it would move, but the ones after that came out easily.

Onto the wagon the men loaded the blocks of ice, trying to keep them in the same order in which they had been lifted from the pond so that later in the day, when they loaded them into the ice-cave, they would fit together as snug as pieces of a puzzle. Air melts ice, and the more closely the blocks fit together, the longer the ice would last.

When the wagon bed was full of ice, the harvest crew drove back home to the ice cave, an area dug out of the ground much the same as the root cave near-by. Naturally insulated by the ground, the underground room was cool all year long, but to make sure, the farmers used other insulation as well. Those who lived near saw-mills -- and there were many small water-powered ones throughout the state on streams near groves of trees -- used clean sawdust; others used straw or prairie hay.

The youngest child in the crew had the assignment of keeping the trap-door open so that the bigger brothers could carry the blocks of ice down the steps to the cave. There they loaded the ice, packing the blocks tightly together. When the first layer was laid in, they covered it with sawdust or straw, then laid another layer of ice blocks, loading the cave layer by layer until it was filled to the ceiling. Then they closed the door to the cave, went back up the steps and closed the trap-door, brushing their hands at the completion of yet another job.

The crew knew that in months to come the ice would be used to make rich creamy ice cream for Sunday dinner, to stock the wooden ice-box in the kitchen or on the back porch to cool milk and other perishables, and to cool freshly butchered meat while it hung. The ice put down during the coldest days of winter would last for a year, even through the hottest days of next July and August.

The ice cave served them well, even at times as a hideout for moonshine during prohibition years. But it was to be two or three generations before Nebraskans learned the pleasures of tinkling ice-cubes in tea or drinking water; the natural ice from the pond was unsafe for drinking, suitable only for cooling.

18

DISEMBARKING ALONG THE BURLINGTON ROUTE

The Germans from Russia

By the thousands they came into Nebraska between 1870 and 1920, these families of foreigners who called themselves Germans although they came from Russia and were four or five generations separated from Germany. "Rooshans", their new neighbors derisively called them, not knowing that most of them spoke not a word of Russian and had always held themselves apart from the Russian populace. Although the 1920 census figures showed that more than fifteen thousand people then living in Nebraska were Russian-born, only a handful considered themselves Russians. All the rest were Germans from Russia.

Their confused status began in the 1760's when Catherine the Great sought out Germans to settle certain parts of Russia to till the land and act as buffers against barbarians. She offered them free land, exemption from taxes and conscription, and the chance to retain their schools, churches, language and cultural patterns. For the next hundred years, they considered themselves Germans who happened to live in Russia. But in 1864, Czar Alexander II revoked those privileges. Since the Great Plains were then opening up for settlement, the Germans in the Volga, Ukraine and other parts of Russia looked to Nebraska,

19

Kansas, the Dakotas, and with the encouragement of the railroad immigration societies they moved again, whole colonies of them, across the ocean to America.

Some settled in Lincoln, either in an area in the southwest part of town called ''Rooshan Bottoms'' or just north of the University campus, the ''North Bottoms''. Some settled in Sutton and in Hastings, along the Burlington railroad; the Mennonites settled in Jansen, near Beatrice, or in Henderson. Most of the Germans from Russia who settled in Nebraska were Protestants, and they settled in colonies, those from the villages of Frank or Kolb, for instance, living in the same Nebraska village, even living next-door to the neighbors they had had before. Their German was a hundred years or more removed from the language the immigrants from Germany spoke, as strange to them as Shakespearean English was to Americans.

Unskilled laborers, speaking a strange language, with large families to support, the new townsmen went to work as manual laborers on railroad section gangs, in brickyards, as draymen. Their womenfolk worked in factories, making cigars or candy or harness equipment, or toiled as domestics, cleaning houses and doing laundry for others. Their children did what odd-jobs they could, and scavenged coal that had fallen from the railroad coal cars (rather than lignite, a particular kind of coal, they called it lug-night for they carried it home in gunnysacks after dark). Families raised chickens, tended gardens, and somehow managed to get groceries for the schnitz suppe (fruit soup), grebble (doughnuts), blina (potato pancakes) and other ethnic dishes that supplied their wants. Much of their social life centered around the church.

In the spring, their greeting to each other was *''Hast du ein Kontract?''* as they prepared to go to the beet fields in western Nebraska or eastern Colorado. In early May, the families boarded special trains in Lincoln, Sutton or Hastings, with enough clothing, bedding and basic household equipment to last them until November. When they got off the train at Minatare, or Melbeta or Scottsbluff, they went directly to the unfurnished shanties that served as their homes. For the next six months whole families worked together, under contract to the grower, blocking, thinning, chopping and harvesting sugar beets under the hot summer sun.

The money they earned during the summer months they applied to their bills at the mom-and-pop grocery stores back in Lincoln or Hastings, and used to buy clothing and other simple needs. They worked hard, all members of the family, and they were frugal; in time, they bought land, much of it the sugar beet land they once bent over to weed by hand.

Their children have university educations. Sam Schwartzkopf served as mayor of Lincoln, and Edward Schwartzkopf is presently a Regent of the University of Nebraska. Paul Amen is director of Banking and Finance for the state of Nebraska, having previously served as president of the Nebraska Bank of

20

Commerce. When George Sauer, a former all-American football player at Nebraska, was head coach at the Naval Academy at the same time Paul Amen was on the coaching staff at Army, the traditional Army-Navy games took on a new aura and rivalry as the Germans from Russia from Lincoln faced each other on the football field. Johnny Hopp from Hastings was a big league baseball player, with the St. Louis Cards and the New York Yankees. Ruth Amen, former college and university teacher is now the driving force behind the American Historical Society of Germans from Russia, whose 4,500 members have their museum and headquarters on the Russian Bottoms in Lincoln.

EDWARD CREIGHTON AND CREIGHTON UNIVERSITY

The Irish

When the Irish jigs start up on St. Patrick's Day, large numbers of Nebraskans are justified in tapping their toes. Many of them are descended from the 11,127 who in the 1900 census of Nebraska listed Ireland as their place of birth.

The first Irish in the state settled in Omaha, then a ramshackle cluster of wooden shacks along the muddy banks of the Missouri river in the mid-1850's. James Ferry, born in Ireland, was the first contractor in town, building the territorial capitol and most of the early business structures, hiring his compatriots as workmen. The first register of deeds was Tom O'Connor, and his assistant was also an Irishman.

Many of the most influential men in early-day Omaha were first-generation Irish-Americans. Edward Creighton, born in Ohio of Irish immigrant parents, constructed the telegraph lines from St. Louis to Omaha to the Pacific coast, conducted a freighting business, established banks, developed the first large-scale cattle ranch in the west, helped organize a railroad, and at his death left part of his fortune to establish Creighton University. His brothers helped operate

22

his far-flung empire, including John, always called Count Creighton after the Pope conferred the title upon him for his philanthropic activites.

The McShane brothers established the Omaha stockyards in the early 1880's, Edward Cudahy became one of the major meat-packers, the Coads owned vast ranch holdings and brought millions of cattle up the Chisholm Trail from Texas. Other Irish entrepreneurs included Ben Gallagher, the Hayden brothers, the Murphys, James Boyd, John Rush, and others who established the dynasties that controlled the wealth and development of early-day Omaha and Nebraska generally. None of them went to school beyond the grades but all were self-taught in many subjects; they were scrappers and they were daring in business.

When construction started on the Union Pacific railroad lines in 1865, Irish immigrants swarmed into the area to work on construction gangs, and when that job was completed, they spread out into the new country to head their construction companies in Lincoln and elsewhere. Others came in to work in the stockyards. By 1900 the more than three thousand Irish then living in Omaha had organized the Cathedral of St. Philomena, several parish churches, and St. Joseph's hospital.

Other Irish were settling in outstate Nebraska, some of them under the leadership of General John O'Neill, the most colorful of them all. He had emigrated to the United States as a young man, had amassed wealth and had served in the Union Army in the Civil War, and then become active in the Fenian movement, an Irish-American revolutionary society, serving as inspector-general, later member of the senate of the Fenian party, and finally president. His dream was to rescue Canada from the hated British, and in May, 1866, with six hundred men he invaded Canada at Niagara, resulting in the battle at Ridge-way, but without support he and his troops had to flee. Four years later, in May, 1870, he launched another attack on the Vermont border, and in 1871, he made another abortive attack against Canada in Manitoba. Each time he was arrested by United States forces, and finally President Ulysses S. Grant told him to stop, that Americans weren't allowed to wage private wars against other countries.

That year, possibly on his way home from Manitoba, he visited the Nebraska prairies and decided that since he could not free his compatriots by arms, he could help them escape the hated British by settling on farms in the west. Between May, 1874, and 1877, he brought in four groups of Irish settlers, totaling about two hundred men, some with wives and children, helping them get established in O'Neill and Atkinson in Holt county. At his suggestion, the Catholic Association bought 25,00 acres of land in Greeley county and more Irish settled the towns of O'Connor, named for the bishop, and Spalding. By the time of General O'Neill's untimely death in 1878, at the age of forty-four years, he knew that many of his fellow Irishmen were free from the British oppressor's yoke.

The Irish

Other Irish settled in other parts of the state, and in time, the landscape was dotted with the spires of Irish Catholic churches, those south of the Platte served by priests from Crete or later the Lincoln diocese, established in 1887, those north of the Platte by priests from the Omaha diocese. Families were large, often struggling for a living; their social activities centered around the church. In the Davey area, near Lincoln, the picnic on the August 15 Holy Day, the feast of the Assumption of the Virgin Mary, was the time of a huge neighborhood picnic, when extended families gathered together. Baptisms, First Communions, weddings, funerals, other occasions involving religious ceremonies were times when the Nebraska prairie rang with the lilt of the Irish brogue. Their descendents have lost the brogue but they are nonetheless proud of their Irish ancestry.

SHORES FAMILY IN CUSTER COUNTY, 1887

The Black Homesteaders

When the first census was taken in Nebraska in November, 1854, shortly after the territory was established, of the 2,732 persons enumerated, 13 were blacks, listed as slaves. One of them, according to legend, was owned by an Indian squaw in Omaha.

After the Civil War, blacks began to come into Nebraska in increasing numbers to work in Omaha or other urban areas, as cowhands on ranches, later as cavalrymen at Fort Robinson or infantrymen at Fort Niobrara.

Some came as settlers to acquire land under the provision of the Homestead Act. These included several who homesteaded in 1871 in Franklin county, hoping to found a village to be called Grant; a group from Tennessee who settled in Hamilton county in 1880, and another group from Tennessee who settled in Harlan county in 1889. In common with many other homesteaders, these settlers seem to have been underfinanced and ill-equipped to handle the first few lean years on the prairie, and their homestead efforts failed.

A lasting settlement was made in 1880 in Dawson county near Overton by descendents of slaves who had escaped to Canada by way of the Underground

Railway. They had prospered in Canada and were able to make the necessary improvements on the land to get their homestead patents after they met residence requirements. In 1905, after a couple of years of drought, some of them decided to move on, to take Kinkaid claims in Cherry county, 640 acres of land rather than the 160 of the Homestead Act. They began disposing of their Dawson county land, and in the spring of 1907, eight families in a covered wagon train moved northward.

The Meehans and their three wagons led the train; Charles Meehan was an Irishman who had married Hester Freeman, daughter of slaves, near Windsor, Ontario, and by the time of the move, they had twelve children. The George Browns, who had also come from North Buxton, Ontario, were part Indian. The Crawfords were also part of the wagon train which moved into the Sand Hills to an area north and west of Brownlee, where the settlers took claims that eventually extended fifteen miles along the North Loup river. In this treeless area, they lived in dugouts, later sodhouses, and began to farm and raise livestock.

Their community, a frame building housing the post office and general store and a sodhouse, they named DeWitty, after the first postmaster; after he left, the settlement was renamed Audacious, and after that, Garden. For their once-a-year shopping, they went to the two stores in Brownlee, or to Seneca, a forty-mile trip that took two days across the hills.

They organized two school districts, #110 and #113, and for a while in #113, Riverview, had classes through the tenth grade. Some of the youngsters later completed high school in Thedford. Later a third district school was organized for both white and black youngsters. One of the families sent regularly to the State Library Commission for books, and when a book of Paul Lawrence Dunbar's poems came, the youngsters could not understand the Negro dialect; one of the fathers had to translate for them.

Other black settlers moved in, some of them having learned of the availability of the land when they lived in Seneca, a booming railroad town at that time. By 1912 there were seventy-nine homesteads in Cherry county taken by blacks, and a thriving colony of blacks near Westerville in Custer county, a total of a hundred or more black families homesteading in the Sand Hills.

In 1910 the Rev. O. J. Burkhardt, a missionary evangelist of the African Methodist Episcopal church, visited the colony and helped them organize a church, located about five miles from DeWitty. The first two resident pastors stayed long enough to prove up on homesteads, and although the congregation frequently did not have a resident minister after that, they always had ecumenical services every Sunday to accomodate the various denominations represented there. The cemetery where many members of the black community are buried is on a knoll behind the church.

Although their lives were full of hard work and little cash, similar in all respects to those of white homesteaders in the area, the blacks found much joy in sports and music. They organized a baseball team, the Sluggers, and played and beat teams from Mullen, Thedford, Brownlee, clowning along the way as well as they played. They broke and rode horses and mules, participated in rodeos, and the youngsters always won foot-races at the Fourth of July festivities. At their neighborhood get-togethers, barn dances, they always had an orchestra, a violin, guitar, mandolin and piano, and they sang with the same spirit with which they played. The Charles Speese family wore out two pump organs and a piano in the quarter-century they lived in their sodhouse in Cherry county, for most of their sixteen living children enjoyed music.

By the mid-1920's, some of the black homesteaders sold their holdings to ranchers and began to move away; others followed during the 1930's, and at the time of World War II. Their youngsters have scattered to all parts of the United States.

The State Historical Society has fascinating reminiscences of the black homesteaders, written by Ava Speese Day and Lena Speese Day, whose parents and grandparents were among the first black homesteaders in Nebraska.

A SOLEMN 1890 MARRIAGE CEREMONY

Mail Order Brides

In the early years on the Nebraska prairie, young women of marriageable age were in short supply.

There were lots of vigorous young men: at first, veterans of the Civil War; later on, young immigrants from Europe, Irishmen to lay the Union Pacific tracks, Danes and Czechs and Germans to homestead and farm, others to ride herd on cattle or start mercantile businesses. It was a young man's world, fellows of 18 or 19 and in their early 20's coming out to the wide open spaces to make their fortunes.

An early-day Lincoln-Lancaster county history reported a need for 2,300 young women to establish homes here.

To take care of the men's immediate physical needs, houses of prostitution flourished in almost every community: Old Hat's in Columbus, Maggie Mustard and Venus Weber in Grand Island, Kate Millett's in Hastings, and scores of others, in tents, soddies, frame houses and elaborate brick buildings. The younger women there who wished to opt for the respectable life could; in almost every community, some deserted their profession, married and became fulltime matrons, housewives and mothers.

28

But most of the young men sought their wives elsewhere. School-marms, nubile daughters of settlers, females of all sizes, ages and descriptions were eagerly courted by young men who wanted to settle down to domesticity. Regular meals, clean clothes, and all that. And sons to help with the work.

One prosperous Danish housewife in northeastern Nebraska who needed domestic help for her expanding household kept writing back to Denmark for servant girls, but almost as soon as they arrived in Nebraska, the apple-cheeked young women were claimed by the young Danish farmers in the area. Finally in desperation, the housewife asked for the oldest, ugliest woman in the village, hoping that finally she could be assured of keeping a hired girl. But even that one was found beautiful in the eye of the beholder; within six months, she too was married, to a happy older Danish farmer who was eager for a bride.

One determined German farmer in Boone county heard that a hired girl had arrived at a neighboring farm; when he went to call, he took the justice of the peace with him.

The young settlers who had come from Illinois or Pennsylvania or Michigan seeking wives simply went back home to look; usually their families were still there and could introduce them to the daughters of friends, and after a few weeks the men returned to Nebraska with wives. Some had been astute enough to carry on correspondence with childhood sweethearts so that their periods of courtship back home didn't need to be time-consuming.

But the young men from Europe had no such easy solution to their dreams of domesticity. An occasional one returned to his village in Sweden or Germany to claim a bride, but most had to resort to other means. And that meant that they had mail order brides. Specially picked out ones, too, not from an assembly line.

Whereas in earlier colonization efforts, boatloads of young women were sent to marry -- in Virginia, New France, the Pacific Northwest -- so that the young benedicts-to-be simply went to the dock and picked out a wife as the girls came down the gangplank, on the Great Plains men had to use ingenuity to find a wife. A few young Jews probably used the services of the village marriage broker, or matchmaker, back in the Old Country.

Most of the young men, however, simply wrote to their families back home, or the mayor, or even the village priest, asking about marriageable young women who would be interested in coming to the New World to establish families. They described their financial circumstances and their expectations, always in glowing terms, and sometimes they sent pictures of themselves, stiffly-posed portraits taken in the photographic emporiums of the nearest town. And usually there was someone in the village who needed a husband, for families were large, often with more daughters than necessary for the local supply of available young men, and the prospect of living in America was alluring. Usually the return letters had photographs in them. And as fast as the young men could gather enough money for ship passage and railroad fare, they mailed back letters with bank-drafts enclosed.

Sometimes the letters were less than truthful, the photographs borrowed. One Czech family promised their 16-year-old daughter but she eloped with a local swain the night before she was to leave the village; the family simply substituted their 14-year-old daughter, who went alone across the Atlantic and onto the Burlington railroad, arriving in Deweese to meet her bridegroom who waited at the station with the priest. He expected a 16-year-old, found a child instead; she expected a handsome 29-year-old farmer, met an ugly 40-year-old one instead. They wed, and when she gave birth to their second child two years later, she went mad and spent the rest of her life in an insane asylum.

Most of the marriages were tolerable, however, and some were happy. There is no way of knowing how many mail order marriages there were. Marriage licenses tell only the place of birth, not the circumstances of the wedding; parish priests in their memoirs do not mention mail order weddings; families either do not know the stories of their ancestors' weddings, or if they do, they won't say. But nevertheless mail order brides helped populate Nebraska a century ago.

CATHOLIC CHURCH IN DALE

Churches

Because the settlement of Nebraska coincided with the mid-19th century religious revival in New England, and because many ethnic groups settled in communities according to doctrinal compatability, churches have always played an important role in Nebraska.

In addition to their ecclesiastical purposes, they also served as social centers, church-sponsored sewing bees, ladies' aid and missionary societies, and youth activities the means whereby many families had contact with others in the neighborhood. Even now one of the first questions addressed to a newcomer, particularly in small towns in Nebraska, may be "What church do you belong to?" Although only an estimated third of the population at any time is ever on church rolls, still church membership is a means of identification.

The first settlers reflected the Protestant leanings of their New England origins. In 1860, six years after Nebraska was open to settlement, there were thirty-two Methodist congregations, fourteen Presbyterian, and smaller numbers of Congregational, Baptist, Episcopal, and Christian churches.

Thirty years later, after the influx of immigrants from Europe, there were 2,979 church organizations of varying sizes in the state, including 387 Lutherans of assorted synodical affiliations and 213 Catholics. Today the church population in Nebraska is estimated at one-third Catholic, one-third Lutheran, and one-third other Protestant.

At first the Lutherans were divided on ethnic lines. The Swedes belonged to the Augustana synod, the Germans mostly to the Missouri synod and the German Nebraska synod, the Danes to the United Danish Evangelical synod (the so-called Happy Danes) or the American Evangelical synod (the Gloomy ones), the Norwegians to their own, each group fiercely defending its doctrine against interlopers. Although in the Old Country, many of them had not been particularly church-oriented, in the New World the immigrants found solace and sociability in their church associations.

The Catholics shared their churches, Irish, Czech, Germans, French-Canadians worshipping together in Latin, although Catholic communities often represented single ethnic groups.

Then as now, churches were busy year long, with Sunday School outings in the summer-time, revivals in the fall, Christmas programs of recitations and visits from Santa Claus. Springtime brought a flurry of religious activity as congregations observed Lent and celebrated Easter. Young adolescents, particularly those in Lutheran and Catholic churches, prepared for confirmation and First Communion ceremonies which marked the end of their Saturday school religious instruction which had taken place over a period of weeks or years, depending on the strictness of the doctrine involved. On the appointed Sunday in the spring, after Easter, little girls donned their new white dresses, and if they were Catholic, white veils, and little boys spruced up in stiff new suits for Confirmation or First Communion ceremonies which were followed by family gatherings, enormous Sunday dinners, and presents for the new church communicants.

In sparsely-settled rural areas, however, denominational lines were more fluid. Almost every neighborhood had its church building, a plain white spired building perched on the prairie, often the settlement gathering place. If most of the families in the area were of the Methodist persuasion, then ostensibly the church was Methodist, although the pastors who ministered to it could vary denominationally, United Brethren, Baptist, Presbyterian, Congregational interchanging without difficulty. A few of the earliest ministers took homesteads and remained in the areas they served but most of them were more-or-less itinerant, serving one small congregation a year or two, then moving on to another, hopefully larger, more affluent one in the next county. Sometimes a single minister would serve two or more small churches at a time, circuit-riding in his buggy or wagon.

In those regions, too, the American Sunday School Union flourished at the turn of the century. Non-denominational, founded by New Englanders to provide religious instruction to pioneer children, the Union supplied lesson plans and scriptural materials presumably for youngsters although in many instances adults joined the classes as well. The volunteer teachers sometimes provided the only religious services in churches which were between-ministers. Within its ecumenical confines, neighbors could learn Bible verses together, whether they were Episcopal, Lutheran, Evangelical or Mennonite.

The Christian Endeavor movement was another non-sectarian organization early in the twentieth century, often sponsored as the youth program in otherwise denominational churches.

It was as a social institution that the church made its biggest contribution in the lives of the early settlers, providing a means whereby strangers of diverse backgrounds could gather together to become friends. The fellowship was far more important than the salvation.

SALINE COUNTY WOMEN SOKOLS IN UNIFORM, 1890's

The Czechs

Fiercely independent with a culture they had protected for centuries from outside influence, thousands of immigrants from the Austro-Hungarian provinces of Bohemia and Moravia streamed into Nebraska between 1865 and 1900. More came to this state than to any other, the 67,000 who were in Nebraska in 1910 representing one-fifth of all Bohemians in the United States.

But they didn't want to be called Bohemians. They equated that word with artists in garrets in Paris, the life of LaBoheme, irregular if not immoral. They called themselves Czech after a sixth century patriot, spoke a language completely different from the German of the rulers who had dominated them for hundreds of years, and when their homeland finally became free and independent in 1918, they called it Czechoslovakia.

The first Czech to see Nebraska was Joseph Francl who crossed it in 1854 on his way to California; five years later he came back and settled in Crete. In 1856 other Czechs began to come upriver on the Missouri from St. Joseph to the village of Arago, thirty miles from Brownville, fanning out from there to settle in areas north and west. By the time the Homestead Act went into force

34

in 1863, sizeable numbers of Czechs began to arrive, some coming from Iowa and Illinois where they had settled temporarily after fleeing their native country following an abortive revolution in 1848. One group of eight hundred came as a colony from Chicago. When the Burlington railroad began to campaign extensively in Europe for immigrants, thousands of Czechs came directly to Nebraska, attracted by the liberal terms that the Burlington offered them. Vaclav Vodicka, its agent in Omaha, was especially helpful to them. Before long, there were Czech communities in Saline, Saunders, Pawnee, Colfax, Dodge, Douglas, Knox and Butler counties, settlers seeking new lands to escape overpopulation and militarism in the Old Country.

In Wilber and Crete, Milligan and Tobias, Prague and Bruno, Clarkson and Schuyler, David City, Tabor, Dwight, Verdigre, the language of the town was Czech, and polkas, beer and expansive family gatherings relieved the tedium of every-day living on the prairie. The Czech love of rhythm and dancing led townspeople to organize Sokol clubs, chapters in a dozen towns at one time providing gymnastic training for young men and women. Sokol halls were combined gymnasiums and town halls, used also for theatrical productions and concerts that evolved from reading and musical societies.

Edward Rosewater, a Jew from Czechoslovakia, founded the first Czech newspaper in Nebraska in 1871, *Pokrok Zapadu* (Progress of the West) in Omaha, and before long there were thirty-three more in the state. Czechs organized fraternal orders; the *Cesko Slovansku Podporujici Spolek* and the *Zapadni Cesko Bratrska Jetnota* were the largest ones, the ZCBJ having 7,095 members in chapters in twenty-two counties at one time. They provided low-cost insurance and sociability, with weekly dances at the lodge for all generations present, youngsters dancing the schottische or polka out of the way of the grownups on the dance floor. The Bohemian Farmers' Mutal Aid Society, organized in 1876, was a crop insurance company with fifty branches and a thousand members before it went out of existence in 1893. At one time there were forty-six Czech banks in the state.

Some of the Czechs were Catholic; some were followers of John Hus, a Protestant who pre-dated Martin Luther in Europe; some were freethinkers. Churches established Czech classes for after-school hours so that the children could learn the Czech language and their cultural heritage. Komensky clubs in thirteen Nebraska communities helped Czechs study their own literature; they were named for the 17th century Czech theologian and educator. In 1909 the University of Nebraska organized a Czech department which continues to the present, as do courses in public schools in Czech communities.

Gregarious and fun-loving, Czechs seized every opportunity for merry-making, celebrating Old World customs, absorbing new country ones, and inventing reasons for partying when there were no others. They love music, particularly bands; Frank Nedela's band in Crete is the first-known one in the state, and it played at the inauguration of the first governor, David Butler, in 1867. Beer gardens sprang up in many Czech villages in Nebraska, and descendants of the first oompahpah band players are still pounding out the beat or playing the accordian when there is no other instrumentation available. Rose Rosicky, Czech historian, estimated in 1929 that two out of every five Nebraska Czechs played a musical instrument. They shivareed newly-weds, celebrated saints' days, and gorged on duckling, dumplings, sauerkraut and kolaches.

Czechs have gone into Nebraska politics: sixty have served in the state legislature, two in Washington, Karl Stefan eight terms as a United States Congressman from Nebraska, and Roman Hruska, a total of twenty-four years in the Senate and House of Representatives.

Although by now the Czechs have become part of the Nebraska culture generally they are still keenly aware of their own particular heritage.

J. STERLING MORTON AND ARBOR LODGE

Arbor Day

When prairie winds waft the scent of apple blossoms or ripple the leaves of cottonwood trees, they carry too the dreams of an early-day Nebraskan whose faith in his adopted land knew no bounds. How pleased Julius Sterling Morton would be to know that Arbor Day, the holiday he conceived and fostered through his lifetime, is now celebrated in forty-nine states of the Union (all but Alaska), usually on his birthday anniversary, April 22.

Born in New York state, reared and educated in Michigan, J. Sterling Morton was a 22-year-old bridegroom when he and his Caroline arrived in Bellevue, Nebraska, on November 30, 1854, after a month-long journey by train, riverboat and finally stagecoach. Twelve days later, young Sterling was a delegate to the territorial convention, starting a half-century of public activities in Nebraska. He was to become one of the most eminent of the group of practical young visionaries who assumed leadership of the territory and the state.

The territory was new -- it had been opened to settlement only six months when the Mortons arrived there. But Sterling Morton could see the fertility of the soil, the promise of the land, and immediately he began urging its use for agriculture and promoting the planting of trees.

The Mortons moved to Nebraska City, took a quarter-section of land, built a modest frame cottage on it which they named Arbor Lodge -- it was later to be enlarged and remodeled several times -- and began to plant trees and shrubbery. Mr. Morton became editor of the Nebraska City *News* and active in politics. He was a member of the legislative assemblies of 1855 and 1857, and was secretary of the territory from 1858 to 1861, serving on two occasions as acting governor, for five months in 1858-59 and for two months in 1861. A Jeffersonian Democrat at a time that Republicans dominated the state, he was an unsuccessful candidate for many other political offices, having been nominated for the governorship in 1867, 1882, 1884 and 1892, and for Congress or the Senate in 1866, 1868 and 1892.

Although public office often escaped him, Morton had tremendous influence within the territory, later the state, serving in many capacities. Early in 1872, speaking to the state board of agriculture, he introduced a resolution that April 10 "be set apart and consecrated for tree planting in the state of Nebraska." He suggested the name Arbor Day, rejecting an alternate title, Sylvan Day, saying that he meant not only forest trees but all kinds of trees, hedges and shrubbery. That year, more than one million trees were planted, and the next year, a like number. In 1874, Republican Governor Robert W. Furnas, his bitter political enemy, declared that Arbor Day be a state holiday, and in 1885, the state legislature decreed that it be on April 22, Morton's birthday-anniversary date.

In 1893, J. Sterling Morton was appointed by President Grover Cleveland as Secretary of Agriculture, and as a cabinet member spent the next four years in Washington. He had spent time there earlier as a lobbyist for the Burlington railroad and did not enjoy the hot, muggy climate, but he savored the political atmosphere. Called by newspapers "Cleveland's Stormy Petrel," he was suggested as possible presidential material, but the rise of the Populist movement and the Free Silver campaign were to defeat any political aspirations his friends had for him. He returned to Nebraska City late in 1896 and resumed work at Arbor Lodge, and two years later started a weekly journal, *The Conservative*.

Although his interests and concerns spanned a wide variety of topics, economic and political, to the end of his life Morton was concerned with the planting and cultivation of trees. With pleasure he watched the spread of his idea of Arbor Day; by 1896, it was observed in every state save Delaware.

J. Sterling Morton died on April 27, 1902, during apple blossom season. He was buried next to his beloved Caroline, who had died on June 29, 1881, and his youngest son, Carl, who had died of double pneumonia on January 7, 1901. His three surviving sons were Joy, who had founded the salt company bearing his name; Paul, a vice-president of the Santa Fe railroad who became Secretary of

38

the Navy under President Theodore Roosevelt; and Mark, who worked in the family businesses but was more at home tilling the soil of his own farms.

Arbor Day is a monument to the vision of a man who understood the importance of trees, and knew that the Great American Desert could be made fruitful.

A detailed story of his life is given in the book *J. Sterling Morton* by James C. Olson, published by the University of Nebraska Press.

DANISH GYMNASTIC AND FOLK DANCE GROUP, OMAHA, 1912

The Scandinavians

Into the rolling wooded areas of northeastern Nebraska, then to the broad flat prairie lands, Scandinavians came to Nebraska in the latter part of the nineteenth century, tens of thousands of them from Sweden, Denmark and Norway.

The earliest Scandinavians in the state came to Omaha as laborers to help build the Union Pacific railroad; later ones arrived as farmers directly from the Old Country, clusters of colonists coming together to settle in an area. The 1890 census listed 24,693 Swedes, 12,531 Danes and 3,632 Norwegians in Nebraska, and by the turn of the century hundreds of Swedish or Danish communities dotted the Nebraska countryside, many of the names reminiscent of the Old Country: Gothenburg, Stromsburg, Malmo, Dannebrog, even Wausa, named after Swedish king Gustavus Vasa.

So fast did the immigrants from Scandinavia arrive, in fact, that from time to time exasperated immigration officials changed their names, declaring that "there are too many Johnsons here now; choose another name." Some bewildered newcomers who had left their Swedish villages with one surname settled in the new country under another one. They were attracted not only by free lands but by freedom, to be rid of repressive social and economic conditions in a still-feudal society.

The land and the climate were different from those they had known at home -- few trees, no rocks, few lakes; the language and customs were alien. To cushion the cultural shock they felt in the flat drylands of the sodhouse civilization, the newcomers tended to settle together in ethnic communities, Swedes with Swedes, Danes with Danes, to read Swedish or Danish-language newspapers, and to attend church services conducted in their own language. Although some Swedes had emigrated to escape religious restrictions which forbade any gatherings not conducted by an ordained minister of the Established Church, most of the Scandinavians in Nebraska were Lutherans, Swedes in the Augustana Synod and Danes in two ethnic synods.

The Danes established their own folk school at Nysted, near Dannebrog, and later Dana College at Blair; the Swedes, Luther College at Wahoo, and a number of Swedish hospitals, including Deaconess in Omaha and Bethphage Mission at Axtell "for those who are in bonds," epileptics.

Scandinavians generally were diligent, hard-working people without outward levity or humor, most of them strongly allied with the Republican ticket although some were Populists in the 1890's. The yarn is told that when a group of Norwegian settlers in Boone county went to take out their first citizenship papers so that they could file for homesteads, only one of them could speak English, and when he asked the county clerk to clarify the words of the oath they were to take, that official, an ardent Republican, said, "You are applying to become a citizen of a republic. Therefore you must be Republican in politics." From then on in Boone county, Republicans could always count on a hundred Norwegian votes. Many Scandinavians in Nebraska have gone into state and national politics, almost always as Republicans. They include Governors Victor Anderson and Val Peterson, the latter eventually becoming a United States ambassador, and so many officials that some wags have commented that "anyone with a Scandinavian name can get elected in Nebraska!"

The day-to-day lives of Scandinavians were not unlike those of other early settlers in the sodhouse frontier who survived years of bleakness, despair, joy, and fulfillment. Their stories told eloquently in a number of books, including Ole Rolvaag's *Giants in the Earth* and *Peder Victorious*, Johan Bojer's *The Emigrants*, and Sophus Winther's *Take All to Nebraska*. Nebraska's foremost musical figure, Howard Hanson, incorporated the Swedish immigrant experience in many of his compositions.

Scandinavian housewives pride themselves on well-scoured homes and kitchens redolent with the yeasty scent of breadstuffs. Their culinary prowess they demonstrate at Swedish smorgasbords in Saronville, Stromsburg and Holdrege, at a Danish Christmas celebration at Blair, and at other ethnic festivals throughout the year, including the Norwegian one at Newman Grove. Although Scandinavian immigrants assimilated rapidly into American cultural patterns, their descendents are now reviving their ethnic traditions.

So significant have the Scandinavians become in Nebraska that for years a sign on Highway 30 on the outskirts of Chappell read, "All Swedes Have the Right of Way."

MORMONS CROSSING THE PLAINS WITH HANDCARTS

The Mormons

The most incredible story of the westward migration is that of the Handcarts to Zion, three thousand footsore Mormons, many of them women and children, trudging across the breadth of Nebraska and beyond, pulling two-wheeled handcarts loaded with their worldly possessions. Between 1856 and 1860 ten companies of Saints plodded through the summer heat thirteen hundred miles to what is now Salt Lake City. They were part of the estimated twenty thousand Mormons who crossed the Plains to the promised land of Deseret, now Utah, during a period of fourteen years.

Shortly after the founding of the church in 1830 in New York state, Prophet Joseph Smith announced that the group would establish its home on the frontier. In 1846, after having been hounded from one place to another, including Nauvoo, Illinois, where Smith was murdered, they reached the Iowa side of the Missouri river, preparing to cross into Indian lands. The government was then involved with the Mexican War in California and New Mexico, and Brigham Young, the new leader, was able to make a deal: he would supply five hundred ''volunteers''

43

for the army so that the Mormons could camp on Indian lands in Nebraska through the winter.

In the area now known as Florence, they established Winter Quarters, more than three thousand pilgrims moving across the river to live in wagons, caves dug out of hillsides, or in cottonwood log cabins while they organized and waited for spring. But they were ill-prepared for an unusually severe winter, and more than six hundred of them died of sickness, cold or starvation.

The next year, in April, 1847, the first group set out for Zion, 148 of them in a covered wagon train led by Brigham Young, following the north side of the Platte river through Nebraska and beyond, as far as they could get from the Gentiles or non-Mormons. From then on, an almost steady stream of wagons rumbled along the Mormon Trail during the summer months, Mormons always traveling together, neither wanting to be with others nor wanted by other travelers. The Mormons were by far the best organized of the wagon trains, formed into Tens, Fifties, Hundreds, each person identified with a specific train from start to finish, all of them supervised with precision.

To increase the ranks of Mormons, missionaries went to Europe and were so effective in their proselytizing that between 1849 and 1855, 16,000 new converts crossed the Atlantic, many coming from poverty and squalor to seek the Promised Land. To help pay their passage at sea and wagon train expenses on land, the church established a Perpetual Emigration Fund, money loaned to be repaid later in Deseret so that no one had to be denied the chance to go to Zion. But the numbers of needy pilgrims grew so rapidly that by 1855, the Emigration Fund was almost exhausted.

Then it was that Brigham Young came up with a daring idea: let the people walk, pulling their possessions in specially-made hand carts. He designed the two-wheeled wooden carts himself, each one capable of holding four hundred pounds of freight, generally one cart to a family. Each person was limited to seventeen pounds of clothing and utensils, the rest of the space on the cart needed for food supplies for the road. He had the carts made in Iowa City, where he also organized trail procedures for the departure point.

The first two companies pulled out of Iowa City on June 9 and June 11, 1856, and on September 26, they rolled down the mountain into Zion, having crossed Iowa, Nebraska and most of Wyoming on foot. By day they trudged across the dusty plains, waded streams, were buffeted by wind and rain; by night they camped in tents encircled with carts, singing such trail songs as "Some must push and some must pull as we go marching up the hill." Those from Germany, Switzerland, Norway, Sweden, even Wales and Ireland, could not talk with the others, but they could sing.

"The carts were generally drawn by one man and three women each, although some carts were drawn by women alone. There were about three women to one man, and two-thirds of the women were single. It was the most motley crew I ever beheld,'' an observer of the day wrote. "The road was lined for a mile behind the train with the lame, halt, sick and needy. Many were quite aged....Some were on crutches; now and then a woman with a child in her arms and two or three hanging hold of her, with a forlorn appearance, would pass slowly along.''

But twenty, sometimes even twenty-five miles a day they trudged at times, their loads lightening as they used up the flour, molasses, bacon they pulled, almost three thousand persons with a total of 653 carts. Two of the companies, those which started in July, 1856, were caught in snowstorms in Wyoming with a tremendous loss of life; many of those Saints were from Europe, for the delay of the ship across the Atlantic had caused them their late start from Iowa City.

As Brigham Young had predicted, the Saints -- even with the very young, very old, and weak among them, on foot -- made far better time on foot across the prairie than the lumbering ox-drawn wagon trains. A detailed account of the handcart expedition is given in LeRoy and Ann Hafen's Book, *Handcarts to Zion*.

DETAIL FROM *PRAIRIE WOMAN* BY ELIZABETH DOLAN

Pioneer Mothers

Heroic bronze statues romanticizing the prairie mother show her gazing off into the broad horizon thinking good thoughts. They give no clues of the fears, the loneliness, the exhaustion and the emotional and physical starvation she lived with day after day in an alien land.

Women who lived in villages and small towns in Nebraska in the late nineteenth century led lives not too dissimilar from those they had known elsewhere. But those who lived in remote farms scattered on the prairie often led lives of bleakness and despair, of terror and loneliness. Their moments of happiness and pleasure were few, their hours of desolation many.

Separated from old friends and relatives, far away from neighbors, prairie women suffered most of all from loneliness. Except for their husbands and youngsters they saw no one, had no one to talk to, for weeks, months on end. Their menfolk sometimes saw others of their kind, either at times of crisis, such as a prairie fire, or in communal work, such as helping with haying or threshing, or in occasional trips to town, a day's ride away, to file papers at the courthouse, borrow money at the bank, or buy supplies of goods that couldn't be raised on

46

the farm. But the women stayed at home and hungered for the sight of other adults, other women to socialize with.

In the earliest days of white settlement in the new land, when Indian uprisings against the settlers were still a possibility, prairie mothers were often terror-stricken when they were left alone with children on the claim while the man of the house was absent. Andreas' *History of Nebraska,* written in 1882, records a number of stories, perhaps some of them apocryphal, of Indian visits to isolated farms. Although most of the visits were uneventful, without bloodshed, the dread of what-might-happen was devastating to the emotional stability of women left behind, often malnourished, usually pregnant, with whimpering youngsters to care for and the chores of the farm to tend to.

In childbirth, the women felt their lonesomeness too, for they had to rely on a neighbor's wife, sometimes miles away by horse-and-wagon, for midwifery help. And the babies came often, every year or so, their arrivals exhausting the women who were already overtired from the rigors of survival in a hostile land of wind, blistering sun, bone-chilling cold.

Those mothers too had to combat the diseases, snake-bites, broken bones, burns, the accidents without number that beset their children. They created their own remedies as best they could, for they had no one to talk to, to give advice, to help them select herbs from the fields for poultices or infusions. And they buried their children. Word of death spread rapidly across the prairie, and unless the death was from an epidemic disease, neighbors from miles around would gather to help with funeral preparations, women washing and straightening the body while men chiseled into the ground to dig a grave. Cholera, dysentery, diphtheria, summer complaint, colic all contributed to the numbers of small mounds adjoining sodhouses or dugouts or other primitive homes on the plains. A poignant story of the death of a toddler is told in *Tales from the Prairie*, Volume 1, published by the Adams County Historical Society.

Devasting though those occasions were, it was the day-to-day living that was the most destructive to a woman's soul. The dreary monotony of constant, never-ending labor -- making clothing from leftovers, making soap from leftover fats, nursing and tending babies, feeding chickens and gathering eggs, helping butcher hogs and cattle, gathering native berries and vegetables, preserving foods in summer in big black kettles in the yard for winter use, working in the fields alongside their husbands -- added to the worries about the mortgage, the unproductive crops, the grinding poverty that seemed to have no respite -- these were erosive.

There were suicides, desperate women drinking lye, slitting themselves with butcher knives, hanging themselves if there was a ridge pole high enough. Others lapsed into depression and even violent insanity and were taken away.

Some women had to carry on as both mothers and fathers. Runaway horses, accidents in the fields, other disasters widowed many homesteading wives who then had to assume all of the responsibilities of the farm, plowing, planting, reaping and harvesting, tending livestock, as best they could. Somehow, they managed.

Through adversities unbelievable, the pioneer mothers survived. They fed, clothed, nurtured their children and a surprising number of them lived to see their children's children to maturity, the human harvest the pioneer mothers had sown. To honor the pioneer mother is appropriate, but to realize the difficulties of her life is to make the honor even more fitting.

DOC MIDDLETON

Bad Men of the West

In the lurid prose of western pulp publications of a generation or so ago, the Men of the West were either lily-white heroes, larger than life-size, or dirty-black villains, evil as Lucifer. In the years since Ned Buntline's penny-dreadful books were published, scholars have sifted through enough evidence to discover that many early-day Nebraska characters were of varying shades of gray. Some were mean and vicious, others weak and only as brave as the guns in their hands, some rationalized that by their extra-legal actions they were righting wrongs. Among the Bad Men of the West, some were shot down, some strung up, and one at least lived to die in his own bed at a respectable age.

Doc Middleton, considered by many to be a sort of Robin Hood, robbing the rich for the sake of the poor, stole horses all along the upper Elkhorn and Niobrara valleys, achieving so much notoriety for his deeds that the geographic area was called "Doc Middleton Country." His motto was to "travel light, travel fast and travel friendly," and many stalwart ranchers in the area sheltered him from the law.

49

Born in Texas in 1851 as James M. Cherry, later adopted by his stepfather James B. Riley, he served time in Texas for horse-thievery, married and begat a child, was a trail driver on the cattle trail from Texas, and along the way, according to the terminology of the times, "traveled under the name" of David C. Middleton, which was later corrupted to "Doc Middleton." He stayed in Nebraska, was embroiled in a murder in Sidney, moved farther east, ran off ponies from Indian reservations in Dakota and sold them, and spread his operations south into Nebraska. Under the name of James M. Sheppard he married Mary Richardson, who was entranced by the slim, gentlemanly stranger. His wholesale horse-thefts aroused a vigilance group and in 1879 he was captured and sentenced to prison. Upon his release in 1883, he returned to Holt county, married his wife's younger sister Rene, and moved back west to Gordon, later Chadron.

He participated in the Chadron-Chicago Cowboy Horse Race in June, 1893, made a living as a saloon-keeper, tried to get into the lecture-circuit and Wild West shows. He later moved to South Dakota and eventually Wyoming, where he died in 1913 of erysiphelas, contracted while he was in jail in Douglas for illegal sale of whiskey. To the end he maintained his courtly manner; A.E. Sheldon, Nebraska historian who knew him well, described him as "having the air of a traveling Methodist minister."

Harold Hutton's book, *Doc Middleton,* published by The Swallow Press, is a scholarly account of his life.

After Doc Middleton's imprisonment in 1879, Kid Wade seemed to take over the horse-thief business along the Niobrara, although he lacked the suavity and finesse of the Doc. Small -- 5 foot 5, about 125 pounds -- of swarthy complexion, he was named Kid because of his youthful appearance. His legal name was Albert. He was adept enough at his business to arouse considerable animosity. He met his end on February 6, 1884, dangling from a railroad whistling post a mile east of Bassett. Later on, his remains were dug up, cleaned off, and his skeleton displayed in the Odd Fellows Hall in Bassett.

Harold Hutton's book *Vigilante Days,* tells more about Kid Wade.

"Wild Bill" Hickok, celebrated because of a romantic story about him in *Harper's Magazine* in the 1860's, was christened James Butler Hickok, nicknamed "Duck Bill" because of his peculiar facial construction, and when he achieved notoriety, the name was corrupted to "Wild Bill." A stock-tender at Rock Creek trail station in Jefferson county, he killed J. McCandles and two of his friends, shooting at them from behind a calico partition. From there he seemed to roam the west, shooting, performing with Buffalo Bill Cody's Wild West show in 1872-73, and finally ending up in Deadwood, South Dakota, where he was murdered in a saloon by Jack McCall.

Homer Croy's book, *Wagons West,* tells of the murders at Rock Creek.

50

The man named Slade seems to have had no admirable qualities. Alf Slade was a mean-tempered superintendent of a stage company, fast on the draw, who became irate at Jules Beni, operator of the trail ranch at what is now Julesburg, Colorado. He offered to cut off Jules' ears, dry them and wear them on his watch chain. Since the Frenchman knew Slade's reputation -- he had by then reputedly killed a dozen or so other men -- Jules judiciously left the country for a while. But upon his return months later, he was stalked by Slade, who did cut off his ears, then tortured him to death with his knife. When Slade was hanged by a vigilance committee several years later, he was still wearing Jules' dried ears on his watch chain.

With brute force, keen eyes and loaded guns, honed knives and ham-like fists, some men of the wild and woolly west achieved fame.

DECORATION DAY IN ALMA, 1882

Decoration Day

Through the years, Decoration Day has always been a favorite holiday of Nebraskans who have celebrated it with enthusiasm, flag-waving, parades and speeches. In fact, the state and the holiday have grown up together, for the patriotic day was first suggested in 1868, a year after the state was created. Many of the early settlers in Nebraska were Union veterans of the Civil War, the holiday was created to honor the Union dead, and on the prairie, any occasion that brought people together was a welcome one.

Decoration Day was the idea of Major General John A. Logan, commander of the Grand Army of the Republic, the Union veteran's organization which became a political force in the United States. He said that graves of soldiers and sailors should be decorated with flowers every year on May 30, with Old Glory flying over them; he wanted "children of the heroic dead to keep alive the memory of the patriotic and dauntless deeds of their ancestors" so that they would "emulate your brave forefathers when the hour of conflict should come for the preservation of the nation, of civilization, humanity and liberty."

Every village which had a GAR chapter organized Decoration Day festivities which started first in the town hall and then went in solemn parade to the cemetery. Even in Gandy, county seat of Logan county, named after the general, the town observed the day with speeches, prayers, music and other suitable activities. The *Gazette-Journal* describing the 1884 celebration in Hastings told of fifty young ladies dressed in white, some representing Peace, others Goddess of Liberty; the drill team in red, white and blue showing their proficiency in fancy maneuvers; and little boys in white stockings, red waists and blue caps with gilt buttons and red and white hatbands, taking part in the mile-long parade to the cemetery, where the youngsters knelt at the head and foot of each of the fifteen GAR graves there and laid flowers on them.

Other participants in the parade included GAR members and the auxiliary; the orators, singers and ministers who took part in the services; town dignitaries and area politicians; and townspeople and countrymen who came into town for the festivities. A leading businessman was usually parade marshal, and the GAR color guard and rifle team had been practicing for weeks.

Since Nebraska City had some citizens who were Confederate veterans, at the first Decoration Day ceremony there in 1883, Honorable George W. Cowell represented the Boys in Gray. By then enough time had elapsed since the end of the war that wartime animosities were largely forgotten.

The services were long; an orator was considered second-rate if he sat down less than an hour after he started. Singing groups performed every verse of their songs; and to make sure the program was sufficiently inclusive, someone was always asked to give Lincoln's Gettysburg Address and many times the Stephen Decatur speech about "Our Country, Right or Wrong!"

As the echo of the last shot from the firing team faded across the prairie, and before the armloads of peonies and mock-orange wilted on the graves, families began to open their picnic baskets. For Decoration Day was an all-day affair; families had driven ten, maybe fifteen miles, for the occasion and were going to make the most of it. The rest of the day was sociable, families chatting together, children romping and playing games, although somehow, Decoration Day wasn't as loose and carefree as the Fourth of July, later in the summer. Apparently the Civil War was more solemn than the Revolutionary War, which the Independence Day celebration commemorated in July.

The May 30 date for the Memorial Day observance took advantage of the growing season; in Nebraska, peonies and "flags," as iris were then called, were usually in bloom, as were sometimes late varieties of lilacs, flowers particularly associated with Abraham Lincoln. (Could that be the reason that two or three generations ago, Lincoln made a deliberate effort to become the Lilac City?) Since cemeteries at that time had little in the way of watering facilities, the flowers on the graves were loose and faded fast. For the occasion, however, they provided color and symbolism.

53

In time there were the veterans of the Spanish-American War to add to the list of fallen heroes. And by then, too, individuals began to decorate non-military graves, those of family members and friends, as well. In small towns, especially, Decoration Day -- occasionally called Memorial Day -- became the time when scattered family members made a deliberate effort to go back home. Decoration Day became a time of reunion.

Four wars later -- World Wars I and II, Korea and Viet Nam -- there are usually military observances at the cemetery, flags waving on veterans' graves. But by now, Memorial Day is a time of honoring all dead, a national day of remembrance.

THE ARMSTRONG HOMESTEAD IN BROKEN BOW

The Boom of the 1880's

Nebraska in the 1880's was a press-agent's dream, a Chamber of Commerce delight, a real estate man's joy. Everything was up, bigger and better and more promising today than yesterday, and who knew how much better it would be tomorrow!

So much rain was falling that everybody believed the brochure that promised "you have only to tickle the land with a plow and it will laugh a harvest," for as soon as the seed hit the ground it seemed to sprout. Immigrants were rolling in by the thousands, tens of thousands, from all parts of the East and from northern Europe. Twenty-six new counties were organized during the decade. The population doubled. Towns seemed to spring up overnight, with merchants selling goods out of the fronts of their stores before the carpenters finished nailing together the backs; storekeepers slept under the counters at night until they could take time off to build houses for themselves.

The fragrance of wildflowers was overpowered by the resinous smell of raw pine sawdust, of soot from the trains that roared in and out of town disgorging new settlers and those just looking. The rough square frame hotels, scarcely

55

sturdy enough to stand up against the prairie breezes, were packed with eager newcomers when the westbound train came in, emptied a little when some of the men boarded the eastbound train a day or so later to go back home to bring the wife and kiddies to this great new land of opportunity.

Those old-timers who had come five, ten years earlier were moving out of their modest original homes into prepossessing Victorian mansions with turrets, towers, fretwork and leaded windows and fancy lightning rods; their wives were hiring as domestic servants the wives and daughters of the new arrivals and using catering services besides to hold elaborate teas, at homes, and other social functions where they could carry their calling-card cases and beaded reticules.

Some of the older, more settled towns were building commercial structures of brick, stone, other fire-resistant materials of size and stability to replace the blocks of dry, jerry-built frame buildings that had burned down. There was a shortage of masons and other construction workers to meet the demands for building the elegant Victorian designs.

Thirty-seven towns had opera houses, imposing structures of stone with elaborate stages, gilt boxes and grand stairways, red plush curtains, symbols of the dreams the towns shared for the future. Not only Omaha and Lincoln, but also such towns as DeWitt, Albion, Clarks, Fairmont, Greeley, North Bend, Madison, St. Paul, Syracuse and Wymore realized the need for cultural growth in the raw pioneer civilization. Few of them ever had operas presented on the stages but everybody called them opera houses anyhow.

There were colleges, too -- not only the University of Nebraska in Lincoln but also private ones in such towns as Fairfield, Franklin, Neligh, Weeping Water, Bellevue, Hastings, Fremont. The number of school districts doubled, from 3,132 in 1880 to 6,242 in 1890.

Fifteen towns had street-car lines -- Lincoln, Omaha, Fremont, Norfolk, Grand Island, Kearney, Plattsmouth, York, Hastings, Beatrice, Columbus, Nebraska City, Red Cloud, South Sioux, Wymore -- and telephone lines were going up to serve customers in most of those same towns. In fact, by 1882 there were even long-distance connections between Omaha, Arlington and Fremont! People in Hebron didn't even have to look up the number of the train station-- it was two-two, and all you had to do was tell the operator "toot-toot!"

The railroads were responsible for much of the frenzied growth. Their lines expanded from 1,868 miles in 1880 to 5,144 in 1890. Not merely the Union Pacific and the Burlington, although they were building branch lines all over the map, but also the new ones, dozens of them, planned to criss-cross the rich farmlands of Nebraska to bring goods in and take farm produce out, connecting every little village to the outside world. The Covington, Columbus and Black Hills railroad, the Omaha, Niobrara and Black Hills, the Kansas City and Wyandotte, the Brownville, Fort Kearney, and Pacific -- they and dozens more went to the communities they planned to serve, promoting the sale of railroad bonds to help finance the construction. So overwhelmed did some communities become at the prospect of the iron rails and so many bonds did they vote that the state supreme court finally had to step in to say that no governmental body could bond itself more than ten per cent of its valuation.

With so much action taking place, it was inevitable that a land boom would erupt. By 1886 it had spread westward from Omaha to Crete to Hastings to Kearney and beyond, escalating, mushrooming. Full-page newspaper advertisements screamed "Land is King!" and everybody ran to buy. In Hastings from January to March 1877, transfers of land entered in the courthouse books ranged from $50,000 to $100,000 per day with lots sometimes being sold two or three times within a few hours, increasing, sometimes doubling in price with each sale. The city limits were staked far out into the cornfields, additions plotted far from town.

And then one day it was over. The hysteria was gone, and there was no sale of land at any price. The speculators took down the stakes in the cornfields or let them rot. Nobody knew why the land frenzy died, any more than they knew why it had started. The boom of the 1880's was over.

ABANDONED SODDIE

The Depression of the 1890's

Maybe they were the Gay 90's elsewhere, but they certainly were not in Nebraska. The economy that had soared to astronomical heights during the 1880's sank to depths so low in the next decade that some of the faint-hearted wondered if it would ever recover.

Ironically, it may have been some of the prosperity of the early 1880's that began some of the problems that erupted later, for the plentiful rains brought bumper crops which in turn caused a glut on the market. No matter how much the farmers grew, it seemed that they seldom had cash enough to pay taxes and the high-priced mortgages with which they had financed their farming operations. The more they grew, the less they had. Wheat dropped from 75 cents in 1880 to 52 cents; corn from 25 cents to 17; oats from 26 to 17. And the railroad freight rates were so high that it cost a bushel of wheat to ship a bushel of wheat to market. At those prices, who could afford to sell? The result was that even before the 90's began, some farmers found it more expedient to fuel their cookstoves with corn rather than paying cash for coal.

Before long, the rain that had been so abundant fizzled out so that by the time the 90's began, the fields were bone-dry. Rainfall that year dropped from a statewide average of 26 inches a year to 17, and by mid-summer the heat had peaked at 115 degrees, twenty searing days in July being 100 degrees or more, shriveling the crops in the furrows. Even if they had saved garden seed, farmers could not grow crops for the table.

The next two years brought fair amounts of rainfall but prices continued to drop, and in 1893, the panic on Wall Street reflected in Nebraska, where twenty-one banks failed, including the Capital National Bank in Lincoln which held a large portion of the state's funds. Businesses all over the state were forced into bankruptcy. By the time the silver mines in Colorado closed that year, bringing hundreds of unemployed miners straggling through Nebraska, hundreds of Nebraska families were already packed up and leaving, those who could afford to feed themselves along the way going back East to relatives.

That year was only a prelude of what was to happen the next year, when a three-day furnace wind from the southeast swooped across the state in July, 1894, scorching whatever growing things had escaped a late frost. Then thousands of homesteaders deserted their claims, wandering to cities in the eastern part of Nebraska to seek odd jobs, anything for a square meal. To add to the hunger, in April and May men of Coxey's Army began to traipse across Nebraska, jobless men from the West Coast making their way on freight trains and on foot to Washington to demand relief. They too were hungry.

Small towns had whole streets of houses with boarded-up windows, and newspaper columns were filled with advertisements of mortgage foreclosures and sheriff's sales. Many of the people who stayed did so because they did not have the physical strength or financial resources to leave.

Had it not been for massive infusions of aid from Relief and Aid Societies, many of them church-related, many Nebraskans could not have survived. Trains brought food and missionary barrels of clothing from the East, and somehow people existed.

In this atmosphere of hopelessness, a new political philosophy evolved. Because much of Nebraska had been settled by Union veterans who gave allegiance to the party of President Lincoln, the state had always been strongly Republican. But by 1890, many farmers began to equate their ill-fortune to the railroads which charged them exorbitant freight rates, were monopolistic in their control of grain elevators as well as transportation, and did not have to pay the same high taxes for farmland that farmers did. People resented the banks and their high interest rates. They were disenchanted with the political structure that encouraged these business activities.

In the early summer of 1890, members of the Farmer's Alliance, the Green-back Party and the Anti-Monopoly League joined forces and in less than thirty days collected fifteen thousand signatures calling for a People's State Independent convention. Eight hundred delegates representing seventy-nine counties met at Bohanan's Hall in Lincoln on July 29 to organize the People's State Independent Party, known thereafter as the Independent or Populist Party. They listed their grievances against the railroad, the elevators and the stockyards, drafting a platform that called for government ownership of railroad and telegraph lines, free coinage of silver, abolition of land monopoly, tax reform and an eight-hour day for all except agricultural workers. During the summer, because there was no farm work to do, they went from one political gathering to another, making a gala occasion of their campaigning. At elections in November, they won control of the state legislature which in the next session passed a number of laws inspired from the Populist platform.

Although the Populists were never able to get complete control of the Nebraska state government, such was their strength that many of the reforms they advocated were later adopted, no matter what political party was in office. Even after the rains came and business generally looked up, many Nebraskans continued to espouse Populist ideas.

THE SILVER-TONGUED ORATOR ON THE POLITICAL STAGE

William Jennings Bryan

Out of the Populist movement that spread across the Great Plains in the 1890's emerged a man who was to have a profound effect upon the state and the nation for years to come. William Jennings Bryan, the Silver-Tongued Orator of the Platte, captured millions of persons through his persuasive oratory and his personal magnetism on the political stage and later on chautauqua platforms all over the country.

Three times nominated for the presidency of the United States and once for the senatorship from Nebraska, he won elections only to two terms in the House of Representatives while still in his political youth. He achieved fame as a statesman, the Sage of Middle America, the Defender of the Common Man.

Born in Salem, Illinois, a graduate of Illinois College and the Union College of Law, Bryan came to Lincoln in 1887 as a 27-year-old lawyer. Three years later he was swept into the vortex of the rising Populist movement. He was elected to the House of Representatives on the Democratic ticket in his first political try, re-elected two years later, and never again won an election. But his fame spread and his influence was tremendous.

Upon his defeat for the Senate in 1894, he became editor-in-chief of the Omaha *World-Herald* for two years, and in 1896 he began to espouse again the cause of free and unlimited coinage of silver, a belief he had vigorously supported in Congress as the cure for troubles plaguing farmers and industrial workers. His dramatic Cross of Gold speech at the Democratic convention of 1896 in Chicago assured him of the Democratic nomination for the presidency even though he was only 36 years of age.

"You shall not press down upon the brow of labor this crown of thorns," he rang out, "you shall not crucify mankind upon a cross of gold." Later that same year the Populists also nominated him, so that he was the candidate for two political parties for the same position the same year, but with different vice-presidential candidates as running-mates. Despite a strenuous campaign of more than 600 speeches in a tour of more than 18,000 miles, despite having garnered more popular votes than any previous candidate, he was defeated.

During the Spanish-American War he was a colonel with the 3rd Nebraska volunteers but saw no active duty.

In 1900, still the controlling force of the Democratic party, he was nominated again to the presidency and again he was defeated by William McKinley. Returning to Lincoln, he established a newspaper, *The Commoner,* which was to achieve wide readership, and settled down in his home, Fairview. He took an active part in the 1904 Democratic convention, helping frame the platform, and in 1905-1906 went on a round-the-world trip, being acclaimed in London as the great American orator. By this time he was participating actively in chautauqua programs which brought culture, entertainment and enlightenment to the hinterlands.

Bryan was nominated again to the presidency in the 1908 Democratic convention, and this time he was defeated by William Howard Taft. In 1912, Bryan announced that he was not a presidential candidate but he attended the Democratic convention, dictated the platform, and was influential in the nomination of Woodrow Wilson for the presidency. In recognition of his service, Wilson appointed him secretary of state.

As a cabinet member, Bryan was able to bring unity to the administration in the first part of Wilson's presidency so that reform legislation could be enacted. Although Bryan's interests heretofore had not been in international affairs, he studied conscientiously, particularly on treaty negotiations to prevent war. Both he and Wilson were opposed to intervention in Latin-American affairs, and in 1914 Bryan supported repeal of the Panama canal tolls bill which excluded American shipping from the payment of fees. After the outbreak of World War I, he was concerned about keeping the United States out of war, and in 1915, rather than sign a strongly-worded note to the German government, the second note condemning the sinking of the *Lusitania,* he resigned; he felt that it would lead to his country's involvement in the war.

He returned to the editorship of *The Commoner* and to the chautauqua platform, continuing to promote the reforms he had long supported. Handsome, with great personal charm, he was idolized by the masses for whom he spoke, the champion of the Common Man. He was a stern, moral man of deep fundamentalist religious beliefs; in 1925 he undertook the prosecution of J.T. Scopes, charged with teachings contrary to a literal interpretation of the Bible. In the July heat of Dayton, Tennessee, he battled Clarence Darrow in court, and five days after he won the court case, he died in his sleep at the age of 65.

Although Bryan was never elected to the high public office he sought, he lived to see that many of the reforms he advocated were adopted: women's suffrage, prohibition, popular election of senators, income tax, requirements of publication of ownership and circulation of newspapers, the creation of the department of labor. He was one of the most influential men of his generation in the United States.

WEST BRANCH CHAUTAUQUA SOCIAL LIFE

Chautauqua

Culture, companionship, chautauqua -- the three words were synonymous in Nebraska seventy, eighty years ago. They evoked mental images of tent communities, orators describing the Holy Land or the evils of drink, band concerts, flags waving, the voice of William Jennings Bryan ringing out across the prairie, shimmering waves of summer heat. For generations living before radio and television dials provided instant entertainment, week-long chautauqua provided the only means of enlightenment and mental stimulation to settlers scattered throughout the Great Plains. In Nebraska, chautauqua reached its peak.

The name itself comes from a resort community in New York State where, in 1875, a summer program of lectures, sermons and music for Methodist Sunday school teachers attracted such enthusiastic audiences that within a few years similar programs sprang into existence for the public in other parts of the country.

On June 26, 1883, the first chautauqua program in the state opened in Crete. The next year the association acquired 109 acres along the Blue River and by the summer of 1885 had two lecture halls and a dining hall built, seven

64

hundred trees set out, and a bridge installed. Special trains brought culture-hungry participants from Wymore, Lincoln and Hastings, and one delegation came all the way from Chadron to live in the tent city to hear the ten-day series of inspirational lectures, lantern-slide illustrated travelogs and musical concerts. One day in 1888, 16,000 persons streamed onto the camp grounds which by then included croquet grounds, lawn tennis courts, boating facilities, and fireworks at night. The Crete chautauqua was considered the greatest conference in Mississippi Valley.

The success of the Crete chautauqua encouraged businessmen in Beatrice to start a similar enterprise, and on June 28, 1889, the first Beatrice chautauqua opened at the new Chautauqua Park which had been equipped with an amphitheatre, band stand and boat houses. The street railway extended its track to the grounds so that horse-cars could run from the center of town to the gate of the chautauqua grounds; the railroads gave discounts on excursion trains to the Interstate Chautauqua, as it was called, to attract audiences from Iowa, Missouri, Kansas and Colorado as well as Nebraska.

In 1907 Hastings established a chautauqua with a permanent pavilion and the other usual accoutrements, the local newspaper publishing tent numbers of the families who had rented association-owned tents for the week so that local stores could deliver groceries and other goods to the tenters and families could locate their friends for sociability.

The Lincoln chautauqua was called the Epworth Assembly and was a direct reflection of the Chautauqua Institute in New York state. Most of the early chautauqua programs were patterned after the original institute, serving heavy doses of Protestant Bible study, philosophy and morality, interspersed with so-called humorous sketches, crayon talks, patriotic exhortations, always travelogues, and music, either vocal or instrumental. Among the most popular of the chautauqua speakers were William Jennings Bryan, Senator Robert LaFollette, Lincoln McConnell, Sam P. Jones; they had to be strong of voice and sound of wind in pre-loud speaker days to be heard in the huge tents that flapped in the Nebraska summer breezes. Madame Ernestine Schumann-Heinck with her big contralto voice was a favorite singer.

Other chautauqua programs sprang up, in Geneva, Fullerton, Hebron, Long Pine, Osceola, other towns, tent cities blossoming in picnic spots or pastures for week-long periods in the summer time, the biggest tent serving as the pavilion, smaller tents as dining halls and junior chautauqua centers for children, and scores of smaller tents to house the eager audiences who flocked in from miles around to absorb culture for a week or two. Hundreds of other families in the neighborhood drove in by day, returning home to farm chores by night, their minds crammed with the wonders they had heard.

The schedule was much the same for all sessions, with programs in the afternoon and evening, all of them uplifting and educational, and special children's programs in the mornings and afternoons. On Sundays some churches in town cancelled their services so that parishioners could attend chautauqua.

After 1900 many small town chautauquas were part of the circuits established by professional promoters who supplied touring groups who moved from town to town to provide most of the entertainment and culture. Standard Chautauqua & Lyceum System and Redpath were two of the largest, utilizing faculty members and students from the University of Nebraska for many of the lectures and musical performances. The circuit chautauqua emphasized entertainment more than serious lectures or debates on politics and sociology.

By the time of World War I, chautauqua was beginning to dwindle in importance as other means of diversion and education evolved: early-day motion pictures, crystal-set radios, automobiles. Although it continued in smaller towns until well into the 1920's, significance of chautauqua on the Nebraska scene then was not great. But while it lasted, chautauqua performed an important service to the people of Nebraska.

FIRING THE OLD BROWNVILLE CANNON

The Fourth of July

Flags fluttered in the breeze, cannonade booms and firecracker bursts fractured the peace, the acrid smell of powder hung over the countryside. Youngsters jumped up-and-down and squealed, babies cried, family dogs cowered, and orators tested their vocal cords. It was Independence Day, the greatest day of the year, anticipated eagerly from one summer to the next by German- and Czech- and Swedish-speaking immigrants as well as displaced Ohioans, New Yorkers and Pennsylvanians on the Nebraska prairie.

Although it is still celebrated, in yesterday's world the Fourth of July was a monumental occasion, the holiday that united strangers of varying backgrounds into a patriotic community noisily celebrating the Land of the Free and Home of the Brave. It was an all-day picnic in a grove, often preceded by a parade with bands playing, floats rolling. Hundreds or even thousands of settlers from miles around gathered by horse-and-wagon to participate in the sack races, tug-of-war, flagpole shinnying and other games; to unload the heavy hampers of country-style food they had brought from home and to gorge themselves on fried chicken, ham, cole slaw and baked beans, before settling down to listen to the impassioned hour-long addresses of the politicians, longer if it were an election year; to recite the Declaration of Independence and give thanks to Valley Forge; to Fire the Anvil.

Firing the anvil was the high point of the day, a deliciously dangerous undertaking. Men hauled two anvils of similar size from a blacksmith shop or near-by farm, setting one on a huge tree-stump. On it they placed a four-inch tall metal collar the width of the anvil face, and into the collar they poured a quantity of black powder, patting the unstable substance gingerly in place and laying a rag over it to keep it from blowing. They inserted a long fuse into the powder, then inverted the other anvil on top of the collar. While everybody stepped far, far back from the scene, one brave man lit the fuse and ran. Moments later, with an enormous boom and clouds of black smoke the powder exploded, lifting the top anvil four, five feet up into the air, and while the crowd cheered, the anvil sailed back to the ground, landing with a thud near the log.

In some communities the men lit the cannon on the courthouse lawn to celebrate the occasion, but firing the anvil was the favored custom in Nebraska for Independence Day.

Later in the day the men joined horseshoe-pitching contests, baseball games, sometimes even a liar's contest. In Crete in 1870, Dick Cater made sure his saloon was well-stocked for the Fourth of July, even though it didn't have a roof on yet.

When night fell, the pyrotechnics began. During the day youngsters had shot their noisemakers -- butterfingers, torpedos, cherry bombs, zebras, block-busters, ladyfingers -- but at night while women and the littlest children watched, men and boys fired the Roman candles, sky rockets, pinwheels and more elaborate fireworks into the sky. When the last spark died, families collected their young, hitched up the teams, and drove home, happily exhausted from the best day of the year.

In later years communities banded together for sophisticated firework displays; Juniata in 1881 spent $250 for fireworks which undoubtedly included such extravaganzas as Niagara Falls and Catherine wheels and ended with Old Glory.

In preparation for the Fourth of July, youngsters saved their pennies for months so they could go to the corner grocery to buy a quarter's worth of explosives, and by the last days of June they began the barrage. Unable to contain their enthusiasm any longer, boys and boys-at-heart lit the punk to fire just a few, a butterfinger inside a condensed milk can, for instance, to see how far the can would fly, and then a two-incher in a can for scientific or comparative purposes, and then compared soup cans to condensed milk cans to no cans at all, until a whole dime's worth of ammunition was gone. In the 1920's, butterfingers were 30 to a pack, five packs for ten cents.

By the first of July in particularly noisy neighborhoods, Rover, Shep and other family dogs disappeared, their sensitive ears assaulted beyond endurance by the bombardment. After the Fourth, they usually returned.

Injuries were common. Mothers kept sweet butter close at hand for burns. In 1915, in Hastings, 12-year-old Lawrence Carroll had his skull fractured by a fragment from a firework, and in 1920, 11-year-old Eugene Douglas had his right hand blown off and his two buddies had serious burns to their eyes when a firecracker detonated. Through the years throughout the state, there were many others, blindings, maimings, and an occasional death.

Little by little, Fourth of July celebrations were shortened so that they were no longer all-day affairs. Air-conditioning and television made people reluctant to leave home, laws prohibiting many kinds of fireworks lessened enthusiasm for the day. The Fourth of July now has become less of a patriotic community activity and more of a family event.

AGENTS MISS HILL & MR. TICE ACCOMPANYING A GROUP OF ORPHANS TO THE MIDWEST

Orphan Trains

When the lonesome wail of the steam locomotive whistle hung on the prairie air seventy, eighty years ago, sometimes it announced that the orphan train was on its way. Over a period of five decades, from the 1870's until well into the 1920's, one hundred thousand homeless, unwanted children were sent from the crowded streets of New York City to small towns in the prairie states, thousands of them to Nebraska.

Babies, toddlers, adolescents, all of them abandoned by their parents, they were shipped west by the carload by the Children's Aid Society, a Protestant group, or the New York Foundling Hospital, a Catholic institution, or other organizations which gathered in some of the estimated ten thousand street urchins or hundreds of newborn babies left to die each year on the streets of New York City. In the newly-developing West, it was thought, they could find homes, jobs, security.

In 1876 the New York Foundling Hospital began sending babies westward, fifty of them at a time. Twice a year, two nuns escorted a carload of babies to be placed in homes in Iowa, Nebraska, Kansas, the Dakotas, the special baby trains, wheels silenced and bells muffled, stopping along the way so that fresh supplies of milk and clean diapers could be put aboard. The trains made pre-arranged stops -- at Greeley, Spalding, O'Neill, Grand Island, Wood River, for instance -- where local priests and parishioners had arranged homes for the babies, many of whom had tags with numbers on them attached to their clothes, identical to the tags the new parents also had as their claim-checks. Leftover babies were placed in cribs at the back of the church so that after Mass was over, church-goers could choose babies to take home with them. Many of the babies were later legally adopted by their new families.

Not so the older children. Few of them even went by the surnames of their foster parents. Boys big enough and strong enough to provide free farm labor were much in demand, as were girls who were old enough to help farm wives in the endless chores of housewifery. Few of these older children were spoken for in advance; when they arrived in a town -- Hebron, Exeter, Sutton, York, for instance -- they lined up and the prospective foster parents looked them over and made their selections.

A Hebron newspaper account in 1890 described the scene after orphans arrived from the Children's Aid Society of New York. ''The (Christian) church was full of people eager to see the children...The selection of children was made by those who had filed applications with the committee. There was not a dull, apathetic boy in the lot. All were bright and self reliant and most of them had good faces. The greatest contest was for the possession of a sweet-faced modest girl of fourteen. There were as many as a dozen wanted her.'' How the selection was made was not recounted, but the names, ages, and placements for nineteen of the youngsters were given. Their ages ranged from eight to nineteen years.

''There were three others overlooked in the distribution but Mr. Tice (the agent) will probably have no difficulty in finding them homes,'' the account said. (The entire story is reprinted in the Hebron *Journal Register* of January 9, 1980.)

Although in some communities the children were lined up on the courthouse steps for the selection process, placements were sponsored by churches, the assumption being that church members would treat their new charges with Christian charity. (Some did.) Youngsters not chosen in one town were put back on the train to go to the next stop where they lined up again for inspection.

Some families chose children for the free labor they afforded, a few for companionship for their own children. Some older couples took girls so they would have someone to look after them in their old age. Henrietta Wiens was chosen by a 60-year-old couple in Exeter, as was Mary Keller in Lawrence, whose new family had lost their youngest son earlier in an accident; Toni Weiler's new parents in McCook were in their late 40's when they chose their two-year-old foster daughter.

The long railroad trip to the West was so traumatic that even those who were very young at the time still recall vividly the agony of worry about their fate. Henrietta Wiens was five years old, the youngest of her group in 1902, so apprehensive she vomited on the fourteen-year-old boy who was assigned to keep track of her on the train; he however felt no malice, bought her a present later with his own first earnings, but neither she nor her new family was able to stop the beatings which his new family administered to him regularly after both were placed in homes in Exeter. Mary Keller recalls that she was one of the last three girls on her train, wondering if anyone would ever pick her. Somehow Toni Weiler knew, even as a two-year-old, that McCook was the last stop scheduled for her train and she still remembers, sixty-eight years later, how she worried what would happen if nobody there wanted her either.

Some children were in family groups. Brothers and sisters were supposed to be placed in the same town if possible. At nine years of age, Larry Davis was the oldest of his family of four abandoned children; one sister, sick at the time the train left the orphanage, was not sent on the train, but he came with another sister and a brother; the baby sister went to a family in near-by Gresham. On the other hand, two boys in Spalding, reared by the Joe Keber family as twin brothers, learned in adulthood that they were not even related. But the three boys taken by John Page in Nelson knew that they were not brothers; they arrived on separate trains in different years, always went by their legal names. The youngest, 83-year-old Fred Fettes, still lives in Nelson.

By the thousands they came to Nebraska, these neglected, unwanted children whose stories provide a dramatic chapter in the story of the settling of the West. Most found a measure of security, a few found love and happiness.

ONE-EYED JESSE HAND WHEN A YOUNG ORPHAN AND IN 1915 WITH HIS OWN FAMILY

How the Orphans Fared

How did the orphans fare, those waifs abandoned on the streets of New York City who were transplanted by trainloads to Nebraska two or three generations ago?

Many of them found themselves treated differently from their playmates on the prairie, ostracized from them, not allowed to play with them. Whether the orphans were legally adopted, taking the names of their new parents, or simply assigned on a more-or-less permanent basis to families, the youngsters discovered a distinct barrier between themselves and other children in the neighborhood.

The attitude was deliberate on the part of the persons who reflected the Victorian philosophy that children of unknown parentage, especially those whose parents presumably were unmarried, had tainted blood and that the sins of the parents would be transmitted to the children. The babies were considered illegimate; they embodied sin. Other youngsters, older ones whose natural families had been dissolved through death, desertion or abandonment, were likewise scorned because -- well, anybody who would do that to a child obviously was not of Good Stock!

A number of orphans still living, now in their 70's or 80's, remember with bitterness that other children were not allowed to play or associate freely with them,

73

and that when the orphans grew into adolescence, they were discouraged from dating in the community. A number of girls, adopted by older couples to care for them in their old age, recall that they were constantly reminded that they were not to plan on having lives of their own, that their present stations in life were prepayment, as it were, for the care they were committed to give their foster parents later.

Few among the boys who were taken in to provide free labor on farms ever were adopted nor did they share in any inheritance upon the death of their foster parents. Some were physically maltreated, beaten more severely than the natural children in the family in a day when might-made-right. Larry Davis of Osceola remembers being ordered to split a pile of wood while the family was away visiting, even though he was ill with pneumonia at the time; other accounts about others of the orphans refer to frequent physical violence. One boy, taken into a family of five daughters, spent his years working on the farm with the verbal assurance that at least a part of it would be his when the parents died; years later when the will was read he learned that he had been left with nothing. When his foster sisters took possession of the farm, he was put off the land he had tended for years.

A few of the children could not adjust to their new surroundings and were sent back to the orphanage; families taking them were given a period of grace during which they could return them. One was a girl who came on one of the four trains from the New York Foundling Hospital in 1912; she was mentally retarded. There was little pre-screening of the children before they left the orphanage; if they were well at the time and seemed capable of doing hard work they were shipped Out West. For the most part, the selection of the individual youngsters was up to the families who had to make judgments on the spot as the children were lined up for inspection.

But grim though many of the stories were, most of the orphans realized that they were better off on the prairie than they would have been back home, wherever that was. Even when they were given a chance to return -- and some of the boys were -- few did so. A boy from Exeter, beaten and removed from his foster home by authorities, could have gone back to the orphanage but he begged to stay on in Nebraska; he worked his way through high school and college, later becoming a high school superintendent in Nebraska.

On the other hand, however, some of the youngsters were treated with compassion and love, particularly the girls who were taken by spinsters or childless couples who treated them as daughters. Henrietta Wiens, for instance, was sent on to college, realizing after she finally met her natural mother years later that she would not have had the privilege of higher education had she not been one of the orphan train children. Robert Turner, taken by the Robert Wessels family near Franklin, felt that his foster family did not discriminate against him and that the four natural children in the family had the same discipline as he; he was the same age as the youngest daughter in the family and when one was kept after school for some transgression in the country schoolhouse, the other stayed too so that the parents would not be able to assign blame and punishment. Wesley Wagner, taken in by the William Willeford

74

family in Tobias, nicknamed Boots because of the ill-fitting boots he wore when he got off the train, later married his foster sister, Hazel, and became a teacher in Burwell.

Records from the orphanages were so fragmentary and there were so many institutions sending children West that it is impossible to know exactly how many youngsters came to Nebraska nor what has happened to all of them. One became a nun, Sister Mary Raphael; the orphan who considered herself her sister, Thelma Bernhardt Leif of Exeter, was active in community work. Others were teachers, farmers.

In 1962 orphans from one of the Foundling Home trains of 1912 gathered together in Grand Island and have had yearly reunions since. The Nebraska State Historical Society is assembling a register of names from the orphan trains which once chugged to stops in small towns in Nebraska with their cargoes of homeless children.

World War I

Incredible as it seems now, America's entry into World War I apparently was a surprise, at least to many Nebraskans. There were wars in various parts of the world, to be sure, but by 1917 the United States seemed in no danger of becoming involved.

The Mexican troubles, particularly with that man Villa, appeared settled after American soldiers, including the Nebraska National Guard, showed up at the border in 1916. Nebraska's Gen. John J. Pershing commanded the U.S. forces, and now the newspapers no longer screamed headlines "War with Mexico Imminent!" as they had earlier.

The war in Europe, with England and France against Germany, which had started in 1914 got scary when some Americans lost their lives after the Germans sank the passenger ship *Lusitania* -- in fact, Nebraska's own William Jennings Bryan had resigned as President Wilson's Secretary of State in 1915 rather than sign the second American note to Germany about the *Lusitania,* thinking it would lead to war. Another American ship, named the *Nebraskan,* was also torpedoed and sunk by the Germans. Before the end of 1915, Henry Ford sailed to Europe

76

to try to bring about peace, including in his entourage two Nebraskans, Arthur L. Weatherly, pastor of the Unitarian church in Lincoln and C.A. Sorenson, an attorney, also of Lincoln. They got nowhere, but most people felt the gesture was a political ploy anyhow; Henry Ford wanted to run for the presidency.

During 1916 sympathies gradually began to swing more and more in favor of the Allies despite the fact that many of the 30,000 German immigrants in Nebraska had relatives in the Kaiser's army. The Irish generally sided with the Germans, for if the British were defeated, maybe their homeland could gain independence. But the Czechs and Poles supported the Allied cause, for if Germany were defeated, their homelands could have independence. Ethnic feelings ran high. Many people, however, felt the war was a European matter, of no concern to the United States.

On April 6, 1917, the United States declared war on Germany. Immediately the machinery of war-time living got into gear.

Congress established the Council of Defense, and on April 25, the Nebraska legislature set up a state council and subordinate county councils which were responsible for a wide spectrum of activities: to act as draft boards, ration boards, financial agents for Liberty Bonds and Red Cross campaigns, to create public sentiment for support of the war, to detect and punish disloyal persons, to suppress criticism of the war, to supervise production of food and war supplies. It was a huge assignment, and to fulfill these functions the councils had unlimited power over the lives of their countrymen.

By the first of June most counties had started taking military census, listing all men between the ages of 19 and 25 so that the draft could be whipped into shape. In the meantime, young men rushed to enlist, many Nebraskans in the 355th infantry and the 314th Ammunition Train of the 89th Division and in Nebraska Field Hospital #1 of the famed 42nd or Rainbow Division. By the time the war was over, 57,526 Nebraskans had served in the armed services, with 1,655 casualties. Capt. Nelson M. Holderman of Trumbull was to win the Congressional Medal of Honor and seventy-eight other Nebraskans the Distinguished Service Cross. Gen. Pershing was Commander-in-Chief of the American Expeditionary Forces and Charles G. Dawes of Lincoln the purchasing agent for the AEF. Fort Robinson was a cavalry training center; Fort Omaha a balloon school.

Those too young or too old for active service were issued arms anyhow as members of the home guard, 15,000 patriotic older men drilling regularly in 200 towns throughout Nebraska, or as members of the cadet corps, boys in junior or senior high issued rifles although they had to buy their own uniforms; they got out of school one period each day to do their drilling. Women too mobilized their strength, half of them signing up for patriotic service. They focused their energies on food conservation although rationing of wheat and flour would not come until the next year, rolling bandages and knitting items for the Boys Over There, putting flags in every classroom, and most importantly, surveying the schools and finding to their horror that more than 10,000 Nebraska youngsters were enrolled in German private schools in the state, mostly Lutheran, and therefore still speaking German. Throughout the state, everybody kept a watchful eye on the neighbor to make sure he wasn't uttering seditious statements or showing signs of treason.

Nebraska farmers didn't need to listen to the exhortations from Washington, "Wheat Will Win the War!" to be encouraged to tend their crops, for the rapid escalation in farm prices sent them to the fields. Wheat which was 80¢ in 1910 was $1.95 in 1917; corn rose from 36¢ to $1.20; and both would go higher. Farmers plowed up pastureland, put more acres into production; in the western part of the state, particularly Cheyenne, Deuel, Kimball, Perkins, and parts of Banner, Garden and Keith counties, they doubled their cultivated acreage, mortgaging what they had to buy more land to cash in on the bonanza.

Although America's participation in the war had come as a surprise, by the end of 1917 every Nebraskan seemed to be involved in it.

The Council of Defense, Book-Burnings

When World War I began, many of the 300,000 Nebraskans of German descent lived in tight little colonies where they spoke German, conducted their business entirely in German, read some of the forty German-language newspapers published within the state, attended church services conducted in German, sent their children to German-language schools. Although many were first or second-generation Americans, they had had no need to learn English.

As war-time hysteria developed, super-patriots came into being, these so-called 300% Americans suspicious of all their neighbors. The local Councils of Defense, set up with frightening powers to detect and punish disloyal persons and suppress criticism of the war, among other duties, sprang into action. They set up files to record every family with a German name and that family's financial ability to subscribe to Liberty Bond drives; fingerprinted all Germans not yet naturalized and urged them strongly to begin naturalization procedures immediately. Clerks in stores were instructed to sell only to persons who could Talk American; telephone calls were supposed to be only in English. The Council encouraged citizens to listen for any evidence of seditious or treasonous remarks in the countryside. They did. Henry Mannweiler of Melbeta, William Volk of Madison county, Harm Meester of Adams county, William Bockerman of Kenesaw, John Steffens and Gus Eisenhauer of Plainfield, Walter Siebert of Scottsbluff, and scores of others were called into state or local Councils of Defense for hearings, sternly chastised, and ordered to buy Liberty Bonds to demonstrate their patriotism. L.H. Kruse of Emerson had yellow paint smeared on his cream depot; in other parts of the state, homes of Germans were similarly splashed. John Schroeder of Lyons was forced to kneel publicly before the American flag and say "God Bless Woodrow Wilson;" several hundred persons watched as an Omaha man was taken from a hotel, beaten and forced to kneel in front of an American flag. Nebraska newspapers published during World War I give a chilling story of suspicion and paranoia.

The Non-Partisan League, the successor to the Populist party, was so suspect, because many of its members were German-American, that the state Council of Defense labeled as seditious a book it was circulating: *The New Freedom* by Woodrow Wilson!

The German National Bank of Hastings quickly changed its name to Nebraska National, and in half-page newspaper advertisements assured the public that all persons involved in it "are American citizens with unswerving loyalty to American policies, American institutions and American patriotism... Each heart throbs and every fiber of their body vibrates with the spirit of true Americanism." Every German-language newspaper had to submit its copy to Councils of Defense for censorship before it was printed; the mayor of Lincoln ordered all German music removed from the program before he would allow the Minneapolis Symphony to play there.

Ministers of German-language churches were ordered to conduct services only in English; many of them had to have their sermons translated for them so that they could memorize them, delivering them to congregations who didn't understand a word. Two who continued to preach in German were sent by the Council of Defense to the district court with the request that their preaching licenses be revoked; a Lutheran minister from Gresham was imprisoned by the federal court; a Gage county minister was called before both local and state Councils of Defense to defend his patriotism. When the Kauf family in Hastings went to a synod meeting in Buffalo, New York, the Council of Defense interrogated the children closely about the reason for the parents' absence.

Schools were a primary target for patriotic surveillance. German was dropped from the curriculum in all Nebraska schools, and in some towns, superpatriots and gleeful students removed textbooks and hurled them into public bonfires on the main street. A committee surveyed all books in the Nebraska Library Commission and recommended that some be removed from the shelves. Faculty members at the University of Nebraska were tried by the Board of Regents in

June, 1918; eleven were exonerated, two chastised, and three asked to resign; the president of the Board of Regents, a German-American, was the target of abuse. Even after the war, the 1919 legislature forbade the teaching of any subject in any foreign language and prohibited the teaching of any foreign language itself until the pupil had successfully passed eighth-grade examinations. This was the law of the state which since 1867 until the war had provided for publication of all official notices in German as well as in English. The law, known as the Nebraska Law, also forbade any alien from holding office, teaching or moving freely about the land. In 1923, however, the United States Supreme Court declared it unconstitutional, an abridgement of the 14th Amendment.

Americanization classes in every little hamlet helped speed the process through which newcomers and their families became assimilated. By the time of the Armistice on November 11, 1918, Nebraska was well on its way to becoming Americanized.

THE HORD ALKALI PRODUCTS COMPANY OF LAKESIDE

The Potash Industry

From brackish lakes scorned by Sandhills cattle, an astonishing industry sprang up during World War I, bringing with it new towns, new fortunes. As fast as the boom rose, it fell at the end of the war, and the potash industry of Nebraska was no more.

Potash is used for fertilizer and in making glass and soap; originally it came from Germany where it was mined from mineral veins and sent to the United States as ballast in ships that took goods back to Germany. At that time it sold in the United States for from $7 to $11.33 a ton. But when the United States entered the war against Germany, the German source of potash was cut off.

Several years earlier two chemistry students at the University of Nebraska had discovered while studying minerals that there were lavish amounts of potash east of Alliance. Although they were not able to interest businessmen in their venture, John H. Show of South Omaha and Carl L. Modisett of Grand Island went into the business on their own in 1911. They learned that Jesse Lake, 330 acres on a homestead taken and later deserted by a Kinkaider years earlier, was a rich pool. They developed a solar drying plant, pumping the water into impro-

82

vised beds where the sun evaporated the liquid, leaving the potash salts to be scooped up, bagged, and sold. Although the Nebraska variety was not suitable for the industrial uses that the German was, it provided the ingredient for fertilizer that was badly needed for farms in the southern and eastern parts of the United States.

But the two potash pioneers did not find a market for their product and the company was practically broke when World War I cut off the European source for potash. Then financiers jumped at the chance to invest, the Potash Reduction Company was formed, and the town of Hoffland came into being, 600 persons living in barracks and look-alike houses which appeared ''as though cut out of gigantic sheets of cardboard,'' according to the Lincoln *Journal* of October 28, 1917. At that time the Hoffland company was producing one hundred tons of potash each day and anticipated doubling that amount shortly. The brine was pumped from Jesse Lake three miles away and piped to the plant. It cost only $30 a ton to produce a ton of potash which brought $100 to $150 on the market.

The second plant to be started was the Hord Alkali Products Company of Lakeside which used brine from Snow Lake and others on the ranches operated by Heber Hord. The legend was that when his father, T.B. Hord, had put together his ranching properties he bought a 4,000-acre one in southern Sheridan county from a Denver attorney. When he discovered a 100-acre lake that was a liability because cattle wouldn't drink its brackish water, he asked the seller to knock $100 off the original purchase price for the right to retain ownership of the lake. Nothing doing, the Denver man said. Less than ten years later, he tried to buy into the potash company. All the buildings at Lakeside, a ranch that covered two whole townships, were painted yellow, the Hord color.

Before long the town of Antioch, between Hoffland and Lakeside, became the potash capital of an oval area twenty miles east and west by thirty miles north and south, located east of Alliance. Of the seven hundred lakes and ponds in the rolling Sandhills area of Sheridan and northern Garden counties, sixty to seventy of them contained potash; eighteen of them on state lands were pumped from one central pumping station and for a while there was a great excitement that the revenue from that particular potash business alone would take care of all state expenses, eliminating the need for taxes.

In 1916 Antioch had a store and two houses; two years later it had a population estimated at 5,000, with two banks, a newspaper, a theatre, and all sorts of other businesses to support the potash companies in operation there. The American Potash Company was the first one, financed by Alliance capital and taking its brine from lakes owned by John and Herman Krause, ranchers who earned almost a thousand dollars a day from royalties. Production from this company in 1917 was ninety tons of potash a day, and one hundred fifty men were on its payroll. The Nebraska Potash Company, financed principally by Colorado capital, took its brine from Palmer Lake and turned out eighty tons of potash a day in 1917. The third company, the Alliance Potash Company, financed by Alliance businessmen, took its material from a lake near the source of the American Potash Company supply; this one was owned by another Krause brother who lived in Wisconsin. The plants operated twenty-four hours a day to keep up with the demand for potash. Workers at the retorts and boilers discovered their gloves wore out quickly from the corrosive action of the potash, and that something in the chemical turned their hair red, but they didn't care. The Lincoln *Journal* opined that "if the industry continues long, northwest Nebraska may be a country of red-haired persons." The potash they produced was shipped to Atlanta, Cincinnati or New York to be mixed with other chemicals for farm use.

Everyone concerned with the Nebraska potash production realized that the lakes were finite, and that all alkali would be taken from them within six to eight years. But the end came sooner than most people had anticipated. Three months after the Armistice, the plants were closed down; the embargo against the cheaper, more usable German potash had been lifted. Late in 1919 and early 1920, the plants reopened again but they were forced to close soon afterward, this time for keeps. Hoffland ceased to exist; Lakeside went back to strictly ranching operations; Antioch shrank so much that today all that is left is a cluster of delapidated buildings. Sheridan county is ranchland again and the alkali lakes are worthless once more.

A POSTMAN'S PREVENTION AGAINST THE FLU

The Flu Epidemic of 1918

Not so dramatic as the war itself but far more devastating in terms of loss of life, the flu epidemic of 1918 swept across the world in the closing months of World War I. When the epidemic was over, months later, an estimated twenty-one million people had died, 450,000 of them in the United States. By contrast, in the twenty months of war, only 53,513 American soldiers lost their lives on the battlefield.

The flu hit Nebraska in October. It apparently had started in May in Spain -- it was called the Spanish flu -- and spread rapidly throughout Europe, carried from one American army camp to another, and from there to army camps in the United States. Soon it was rampant among the civilian population as well. By late summer, officials in Washington estimated that there were twenty-three million cases of flu in the United States, 105,000 of them soldiers, with one out of twenty-seven cases resulting in death. On the first of October, draft calls were postponed and army camps isolated.

On October 4, the Hastings *Tribune* reported that a Kenesaw soldier was said to be desperately ill with Spanish influenza at Camp Grant; two days later

Omaha theatres were "closed with regret" and indoor gatherings of all kinds were prohibited. In Lincoln, with seven hundred cases and seven deaths so far, officials closed the schools. Fairbury closed everything in town on October 10, and on October 14, McCook followed suit. On that day in Hastings there were eighty-one reported cases of flu, one death, and a Hastings soldier had died of influenza at Fort Riley, Kansas.

On October 21, the state board of health ordered that "all gatherings of the people be dispensed with both within doors and without in all villages, towns, and cities of the state, that the schools...be closed, and that insofar as practicable children be kept at home...from this date until Saturday, November 2, 1918." Lincoln health officials reported that half the students at the University were sick with flu.

By then the disease was epidemic throughout the state. No community had enough nurses to cope with the situation; many doctors themselves were sick. In many households so many persons were incapacitated that there was no one left to prepare meals, provide nursing care. Volunteer groups went into action, setting up community kitchens to prepare meals which the Motor Corps of the Red Cross delivered to the doorways of the afflicted homes; other volunteers went into homes to shave men, bathe the ill, and perform simple nursing functions. In some towns ministers suggested turning churches into temporary hospitals.

Newspapers reported symptoms. The "victim could expect to be entirely incapacitated for three or four days, temperatures could run as high as 104 with severe headache, chill or chilliness, pains in the back and legs, great prostration, drowsiness, sometimes nervous symptoms, eyes, air passages of nose and throat affected, and maybe gastro-intestinal disturbances, asthenia being a prominent symptom. Onset is sudden and relapse may occur." The most serious complication was pneumonia.

There seemed to be no specific medicine or remedy to counteract the disease; it was to be two decades before antibiotics were developed. Newspapers suggested preventive antiseptic washes or sprays for the nose, nasal tubes for irrigating the nasal tract, benzoin boiled in tea kettles to fumigate and disinfect the household, or camphorated petroleum applied to neck, throat and chest, covered with hot flannel or toweling. Officials in Washington said that army camps were using quinine to treat the flu but the supply was insufficient and the effectiveness of the quinine was not established anyhow.

The telephone company pleaded for cooperation for so many phone operators were down with the flu that the company could not handle all calls; it asked that phone calls be limited to emergencies and that children be restrained from visiting on the phone.

The Red Cross distributed patterns for making face-masks and when schools were finally resumed domestic science students cut the masks, 4 x 6 inches in size "three to four thicknesses of clean old muslin," enough masks that each person could have a clean one each half-day. All students and teachers in class were required to wear them. After the state health order ended, regular church services were restored in most communities with the stipulation that only one service be held on Sunday and that the congregation be seated in alternate pews. Some increase in flu cases was attributed to church services hastily organized on November 7 when word erroneously got out that the Armistice had been signed. The real Armistice, however, on November 11, was celebrated in most communities in outdoor festivities, parades, bell-ringing, whistle-blowing.

The epidemic continued to rage through Nebraska to the end of the year and beyond. In some communities, merchants were distressed because it kept customers out of the stores during the Christmas shopping season.

There is no record of the number of cases. The Nebraska Department of Health listed a total of 1,577 deaths from flu, 5,878 from pneumonia, during 1918 and 1919. Since many doctors themselves were victims of the flu, too harrassed to keep accurate records, it is possible that many flu-related deaths were not reported as such.

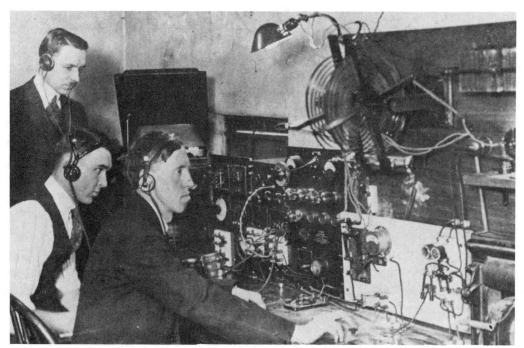

DR. JOHN C. JENSEN WITH TWO STUDENTS AT WCAJ

When Crystal Sets Were Big

When Marconi invented wireless communications, enthusiastic tinkers in Nebraska hurried to put together the coils and crystals that enabled them to hear voices and music from the air. There was much for crystal-set operators to hear from their headphones. The underground water table that supplies life-giving water in the state provides such exceptional conductivity for radio waves emanating from towers grounded there that Nebraska became a leader in early-day radio transmission and reception.

Pioneer radio man in Nebraska was J. C. Jensen, born in a sodhouse in Utica on October 19, 1880, who taught a country school for four years after his graduation from the 10-grade Utica high school, then attended Nebraska Wesleyan University for two years, and in 1903 went to Beaver City as superintendent of schools. During his four years there, in addition to his administrative duties he taught eight classes each day and coached athletics. In his leisure he learned the Morse code from the telegrapher at the Burlington station, and all he could about transmitters. Using window glass, tinfoil, parts borrowed from telephone sets and whatever else he could scrounge, he made a Marconi coherer

88

receiver and spark transmitter. In 1906 the deputy state superintendent of schools, a Mr. Bishop, saw the wireless and asked that it be displayed at the state fair; seeing it there, officials of Nebraska Weselyan offered him a part-time instructorship, at $250 per year, while he finished his degree at the University of Nebraska. He went to Lincoln in 1907, finished his degree in 1909, and became head of the physics department at Nebraska Wesleyan, continuing his work there for the next 45 years. His first transmitting station was 9YD. During World War I he taught radio and Morse code to army signal corps members. In 1921, using the new De Forrest audion tube, he put his campus station WCAJ on the air, the first station in Nebraska to broadcast music and voice. Volunteers provided newscasts, weather reports, educational and religious programs for the 10,000 watt station at 1080 kilocycles. In 1933, the station, now at 590 kilocycles, was sold to WOW of Omaha and became a commercial station.

The second radio station broadcasting in Nebraska was KFEQ, John Scroggin's 12,000 watt station which went on the air in 1922 at Oak. Using books and manuals on electricity, Scroggin built it in the bank, powering the transmitter with water-cooled tubes which cost $700 each. The first broadcasts were from 2 to 3 p.m. and 7 to 8 p.m. daily, with volunteers performing for the pleasure and novelty of the experience. Sunday evening programs were request performances, religious and popular music presented by Mabel and Helen Ludlem on the violin and cello and Mrs. Scroggin on the piano, or by the Schooner vocal quartette, performing numbers requested by listeners who wrote in from every state in the nation and Alaska as well. Afternoon orchestral programs presented by Smith's Entertainers, who played commercially for dances at night, brought replies from sailors at sea. The first radio advertiser was Wilke's Bakery Company of Beatrice; later on Smiley's Hatchery of Beaver Crossing started advertising. They and subsequent sponsors received so many orders from their commercials that eventually they had to drop advertising; they could not fill them all. The station itself became so successful that Scroggin was faced with having to enlarge it -- the tower was in back of the bank, studios in the basement -- and he sold it to a company in St. Joseph, Mo., who wanted it for broadcasting market news.

The next station in Nebraska was KFKX in Hastings, started in 1923, the first commercial relay station in the world for short-wave radio. Established by the Westinghouse Corporation to re-broadcast programs originating from KDKA in Pittsburgh at night, it had its own broadcast schedule during the day. In its first week of operation it received 1,863 letters from listeners in every American state, every Canadian province, Mexico, Costa Rica, Cuba, Guatemala, Brazil, Alaska, Hawaii, China, Holland, Uruguay, Samoa, Australia, France, South Africa, and ships at sea. It transmitted concerts by the State Hospital band, Hastings College musicians and other local entertainers. The first football broadcast was the Thanksgiving Day game between Hastings College and Nebraska

89

Wesleyan University in 1924. An exciting radio romance developed when Dr. E. E. Sheely, a radio enthusiast from Freeport, Ill. began writing Ruth Sherman, a regular KFKX singer, and eventually showed up with a diamond ring in hand; Judge Herman Schroeder, one of the KFKX announcers, proclaimed the engagement and marriage to the audience of ether. Will Hay, another local announcer, went on to greater glory on the Amos and Andy network show. KFKX scored a coup in 1925 when it was the first to interview royalty, shoving the microphone to Queen Marie of Romania as she stopped in Hastings on a nationwide tour. Only casualty of that historic moment was a royal lap-dog; the over-eager announcer stepped on its tail. In 1927, the Westinghouse Corporation sold KFKX to the National Broadcasting Company, and in a few months the station went off the air permanently.

Other early-day stations included KMMJ at Clay Center, named for the initials of its founder, M.M. Johnson; KFOR which operated in a garage in David City; and WAAW, the Omaha Grain Exchange. Nebraska's love affair with radio continues; there are now 57 commercial stations operating in the state.

Porch Swings

Before air-conditioning and television changed the cultural patterns of an entire civilization, front porches were the social centers of the family. In the big book at the lumber yard sixty, eighty years ago, house-plans included front porches, sometimes even wrap-around ones which covered two sides of the house. They may have been called piazzas or verandas, and the architectural styles Queen Ann cottages or bungalows, but no matter the names; porches were the place where the adults gathered after supper on summertime evenings to move slowly back-and-forth in wooden swings, or to rock in wicker chairs, cooled by the air-currents which were stirred by the slow mesmerizing action. The low drone of the grown-ups' voices mingled with the creak of the porch-swing chains, the slap of the wooden rockers, the hypnotic shrr of katy-dids in the trees, the far-off squeals of youngsters racing across the yard to catch lightning-bugs. The adults, two or three to a swing, talked among themselves, sometimes calling across the porch railing to confer with neighbors on their front porches next door.

Sometimes they drank tall glasses of iced-tea or ate huge bowls of thick creamy ice-cream so cold it tingled the jaw. But always they sat. In the hour before dusk

91

thickened to signal bed-time, the family relaxed. Those quiet, somnolent evenings in the summertime were the only time of day that adults felt comfortable sitting for the sake of sitting. Even so, some of the women held needlework in their laps, working on it until the darkness was too dense for them to see their crochet hooks or tatting shuttles flash in and out. There was a comforting regularity to the routine of every-day life.

Early in the morning, before the Nebraska heat rolled in, the family arose to the coo of the mourning dove to perform the heavy chores of the day. Although the fathers' duties tended to be much the same day-after-day on the farm or in the office, the mothers' jobs were compartmentalized according to the day. Monday was wash day, the major assignment being to launder piles of clothing and linens that had collected the previous week; the mother filled the boilers with water to heat, chipped lye-soap into the wash-tub, rubbed garments up and down against the corrugated washboard, lifted them into the washing machine to churn, then ran them through the wringer into and out of the rinse-tubs, hustling to get them onto the clothes line early so that the neighbors could not accuse her of slothfulness. She lifted the baskets to the back yard where she trudged back-and-forth, flipping the heavy wet garments, pinning them securely with wooden clothespins onto the metal wire, undergarments hidden from public view, frayed or tattered wear tucked out of sight of the neighbors.

Tuesday was ironing day, the mother starting early in the morning to sprinkle clothes, boil starch, heat sad-irons on the cookstove, so that she could thump the irons from the garments on the ironing board back to the stove, a noisy, repetitive, muscular job. Other days were for other specific chores: baking, setting sponge for bread, mixing cakes from eggs and butter and sifted flour, rolling pie-crusts. House-cleaning, using wire-beaters to pound carpets dragged to the back yard, scrubbing windows with vinegar water, scouring wooden floors. Sewing, mending, using foot-powered treadle machines. Canning, preserving produce from the garden. And every day there were the usual chores: shelling peas, slivering cabbage for kraut, rolling noodles, peeling potatoes for dinner at noon.

By mid-morning in the summertime, the mother stopped her work long enough to make the rounds of the house, closing windows, pulling curtains shut, darkening the house to keep out the mounting heat of the day. A few affluent families had special summertime decors for their homes: with the hired girls helping, the housewives put away the velour draperies and heavy carpets and substituted light airy curtains and summer rugs, covered the itchy overstuffed furniture with muslin slipcovers. But always they shut out the heat of the day.

Children too had assignments: feeding chickens and gathering eggs, for except in the most urban areas of Omaha and Lincoln, householders kept chickens in the back yard; chopping weeds from the long rows of carrots or tomatoes or beans in the garden, and later picking the produce; emptying the sloshing pans of water from underneath the ice-boxes. Day-to-day living for everyone called for the expenditure of much muscular effort.

By the end of the day, when the after-supper chores were completed and the house was opened up once again to the breezes of Nebraska summertime evenings, the family migrated to the front porch. There with the coolness of evening pushing out the heat of day, the relaxation from physical labors, and the sociability of chatting with other members of the family, the front porch provided restorative powers. It was an essential ingredient of summertime living in Nebraska.

A YOUNG GIRL LEARNING MULTIPLICATION

School Bells

For a century and a quarter, school bells have rung, literally or figuratively, to summon Nebraska children to their lessons. In that time the schoolhouses have changed from soddies to frame buildings to elaborate structures of masonry, metal and glass; students have ranged in numbers from a dozen or more to several thousand in one building to as few as one per school (there are still two one-pupil schools in Nebraska and ninety public schools with five or fewer students). Through the years students have gone to their classes on foot, trudging across the prairie a mile or two from home swinging their lard pail lunch buckets; ridden their ponies to the lonesome building perched in the pasture; boarded clanging trolleys to joggle across town; or clambered aboard buses. Some early schools held classes only a few months a year; now all of them are in session nine months a year and many hold summer classes as well.

Some of the earliest schools were held in settlers' homes, usually one-room soddies or frame buildings, with teachers paid by the parents. As the numbers of students outgrew the size of the quarters, districts built school buildings sometimes of sod. Youngsters attending the Munroe sodhouse school in Adams

94

county had to climb in and out of the window; so eager had the families been to build a school room onto Fred Albright's house they overlooked the necessity of leaving space for the door.

In the one-room schoolhouses that dotted the state two or three generations ago, teachers were often only eighth-grade graduates themselves; in 1918, nine of ten were women, half of all teachers were between 16 and 20 years of age, and another 38% from 21 to 25 years of age. They had to prepare lessons in all subjects for each of eight grades, keep track of the sixth graders while the first graders were reciting, supervise playground activity, serve as school nurse for assorted ills, all for a salary of $10 to $15 per month. They had to sweep the floor, make the fire in the pot-bellied stove, draw water from the pump before they rang the school bell in the morning. They lived and boarded with families in the neighborhood -- one teacher in Hall county remembers dreading the months she had to live with one particular family because she had to sleep in a double bed with the children, some of whom were not house-broken. In the summer the teachers attended Teachers' Institutes to learn new subject matter and new teaching techniques. Often some of the older boys were bigger than the teachers, and older, for some kept going back to school for a month or two each year even after they had finished their eighth grade books.

Country schools, or common schools, as they were called, provided instruction through the eighth grade, and progress was marked by the text-books; as soon as a student finished the first grade book, for instance, he was automatically promoted to the second grade. But completion of the school course was dependent upon the eighth-grade examinations, standard ones provided by the county superintendent. Most of the sixth, seventh and eighth grade work in school was geared toward Passing the Examination, not for the sake of learning.

When the teacher rang the bell at 9 o'clock, the children trooped inside. Those who had ridden ponies had tethered them or tied them to the hitching rail and had seen to it that there was hay available to munch on during the day. The children took their places at their wooden desks, often double ones, nailed together in rows so that the back of one provided the front for the one behind it. Few girl students avoided having their pigtails dipped at some time or other into the ink-well of the desk in back, usually by a playful boy. Those students nearest the pot-bellied stove were overheated, those far away from it were chilled. Behavioral modification was provided by the hickory stick, in Nebraska usually a willow branch or a ruler, applied for disciplinary reasons, and by the dunce-seat in front of the room, where slow-learners or children who had not studied their lessons sat to be ridiculed by the others.

Class by class, the teacher called students to the recitation bench at the front of the room, and while one class recited, all others presumably studied their lessons. If there were eight grades -- and in classrooms with twenty, even forty students, there usually were -- then no class could claim more than one-eighth of the teacher's time. At noon the teacher stopped recitations for lunch. Children collected their lunch buckets from the back of the room, near the coat-hooks, and ate the lunches their mothers had prepared -- huge sandwiches of home-made bread, sometimes smeared with lard, and pieces of pie and other filling, starchy foods. In some schools teachers allowed youngsters to heat foods on the pot-bellied stove which heated the room.

Friday afternoons were special occasions. Instead of classes there were ciphering matches, spelldowns, other competitions aimed at testing children's knowledge, providing motivation for learning on other days. Families often attended Friday Afternoons, particularly if there were declamations or other dramatic presentations. The last day of school, if it were in the spring, was the time of a school picnic, students and their families eating out-of-doors on the schoolground, playing games, enjoying freedom from classes. Many schoolhouses also served as community centers, housing grange and township meetings and even church services in non-school hours.

For its time, the one-room country school served an essential function.

TAKING A BREAK TO POSE FOR THE PHOTOGRAPHER

Threshing

Threshing and cooking-for-threshers were important events to farm families fifty or more years ago in the late summer. Harvesting small grain was not a single operation, as it is now with machines which perform combined functions, but a series of operations spread through the summer. Threshing was man's work; cooking-for-threshers, equally important, was woman's work.

When grain was ripe, about the Fourth of July, the farmer hitched up the horse-drawn binder and with other menfolk in the household went out to the fields of golden grain. As he drove the horses through the field, the machine cut the grain, gathered many stalks together, tied them with sisal twine, and at intervals dropped off bundles of sheaves. Men on foot, usually the farmer's sons, followed the binder to collect many clumps of bundles to stand them, grain-end up, in neat shocks, broad at the base, small at the top, so they could dry. It was hot, dusty, physical labor, but a crew working hard with a good team of horses and binder -- the first ones cut six-foot swaths, later ones eight-foot swaths -- could bind and shock seven to ten acres a day.

After the grain was cut, it had to "go through the sweat" or harden, for about six weeks, before it could be threshed, so that the harvesting of wheat took up much of the late summer.

Threshing was a neighborhood event, farmers going from farm to farm to help each other. The size of the crew depended on the size of the threshing rig; a thirty-six inch threshing cylinder needed ten racks to keep it filled with bundles, and enough men to handle them; a machine with a smaller cylinder required from four to six racks.

The littlest member of the crew snipped twine from the bundles, others loaded them into the cylinder. There the blades cut off the straw and spat it out on one side and whipped the grain from the head, spewing it out a long pipe on the other side of the machine to drop into the wagon standing underneath the pipe. Man-power was needed for all the loading and unloading operations, to rake the straw aside, shovel the grain as it dropped into the wagon. It was a long process in the direct sun of hot summer days, with chaff blowing, dust clinging to the sweaty workers, flies clustering around the horses which were covered with fringed netting to protect them from the horse-fly bites.

When the wagons of grain were full, crew members drove them to the storage area and dumped them. The straw, much larger in volume than the grain, was piled into huge strawstacks to provide shelter and some food for cattle during the winter. Some of it was later hauled into the barn for bedding for livestock, for use as mulch on strawberry plants, for use in mattresses, or for any of a dozen other functions. Straw was a valuable by-product of the threshing process.

Mid-morning and mid-afternoon, the girls in the house were dispatched to run out to the field to carry "eats," thick sandwiches of bread, butter and meat, and stoneware jugs filled with freshly-pumped water, corked and wrapped with wet burlap to preserve the coolness. In the shade of the threshing machine the men stopped their work to eat the sandwiches and to gulp the water, passing the jug from one man to the next.

In the meantime, the women in the house were as busy as the menfolk in the field, cooking for threshers; noontime was dinnertime. In the steamy kitchen they cut up and fried dozens of chickens, peeled and boiled and mashed pounds of fluffy white potatoes, stirred gallons of good rich gravy. They piled onto platters loaves of thick-sliced homemade bread still aromatic from the oven, cut pieces from a staggering selection of homemade pies -- green apple, gooseberry, raisin. From the windmill cooler they brought bowls of yellow homemade butter with their own distinctive design molded on the top; from the cellar they carried jars of homemade jellies and jams. When the long table, the dining-table with all of its extensions in it, was filled with food, they rang the dinner gong.

One peal of the gong was enough; the men rushed from the field, washed their hands and faces at the pump in the yard, and stomped into the house to the dining table. In same workmanlike manner with which they performed in the

98

field, the men addressed the steaming mounds of food, piling plates high and filling them again and again. The hard physical labor of the field created huge appetites, burned many calories. While the women replenished the serving dishes from the kettles on the cob-fired cookstoves, the children watched hungrily, hoping there would be something left for them. Finally the men pushed back their chairs and started back to the field. The women cleaned up the table, washed the dishes, and prepared for the second sitting, when the women and children could eat.

A man was known by the eats his woman put out; if the wife served good, substantial fare, and plenty of it, the farmer found his crew members eager to work.

After World War II, threshing procedures changed. Behemoth implements called combines were added to the machinery on farms, capable of cutting and threshing in one sweep across the field. Instead of weeks, the harvesting of small grain now requires only days, and the numbers of men involved in the process are fewer. Large-scale wheat farmers own their own equipment; others join forces to buy machinery with neighbors and swap services, or use the services of intinerant threshing crews who travel from Texas to Canada following the harvest, doing custom combining for farmers. Farmwives no longer cook-for-threshers; many wives work in town in offices or light industries and members of the combine crew often eat their noon-meals in cafes or fast-food stands. Sitting in the air-conditioned cabs of their massive machines, using power equipment rather than muscles to do their jobs, harvest crews do not generate the huge appetites their fathers did.

AUTOMOBILE DESIGNED AND BUILT BY CHARLES M. FULLER
AND THE FACTORY IN ANGUS

Horseless Carriages

When the 20th century dawned, Nebraska was already infected with a disease that was to become epidemic: automobile fever. For although in 1900 there were only a few horseless carriages in the state, almost overnight there would be hundreds: steam automobiles, electric cars, internal combustion motorcars, hissing and chugging and flapping through city streets and bouncing over country roads, frightening horses, bringing down the wrath of ministers and timid women. Inventors would tinker in their sheds, men would begin to talk about disc brakes, intake valves, and cylinders.

In 1905 there were 571 motor vehicles registered with the Nebraska secretary of state and by the spring of 1909 the Angus Automobile Company had manufactured more than six hundred Fuller cars in its factory near the Little Blue River.

Nobody now knows who owned the first automobile in Nebraska, but apparently the first one manufactured in the state was the Pabian, built in 1897 by Bob Pabian in Prague, a one-cylinder vehicle with a maximum speed of 15 mph and a thirst for a quart of oil every two miles. Pabian never made another car.

100

A few months later Charles Marion Fuller turned out the first Fuller Automobile in his father's blacksmith shop in Angus in 1898, installing a motor with a chain drive in a buggy frame, adding a hand-brake and steering tiller. He sold the machine to a Dr. Redford, then went off to work in automobile factories in St. Louis and Anderson, Indiana, inventing and designing automotive parts. In 1907 he returned to Angus and with financial backing from neighbors opened a factory capable of producing thirteen cars at a time. His model A was the most popular one, a 4-cylinder touring car capable of seating five persons, developing 35-40 horsepower, selling for $2,500. Differences among the stockholders of the company forced closing of its doors in the spring of 1909.

By this time Nebraskans were eager to buy the new-fangled automobiles: Chalmers, Maxwells, Hupmobiles, Coles, Whites, Bushes, Loziers, Franklins, Stanleys, Columbias, Carters, Overlands, Hudsons, Metzes, Reos, an assortment of varieties. And to learn how to drive them. When Charlie Jacobs unloaded his Mobile Steam from the Burlington freight car in Hastings on March 1, 1901, he "oiled the gearing, fired up, and...manipulated the regulating levers with the dexterity of an expert automobilist," the Hastings *Tribune* of the day reported with astonishment. One of his first trips took Charlie past the Presbyterian church in Hansen, stirring up the teams hitched outside so that "some very hard things were said about the automobile by the owners of the horses who were worshipping in the church," a historian reported later. In 1903, the Hastings *Tribune* urged the passage of an automobile ordinance, warning that "The time is not far distant when there will be a score of automobiles chasing around the principal streets at the same time."

Many of the first automobile accidents involved horses which shied and bolted in terror at the strange apparition rattling toward them on the road. When injuries happened they were usually to persons in buggies or wagons overturned by frantic horses. The 1905 Nebraska legislature passed a law requiring the operator of an automobile to halt until the driver of a frightened horse could get past.

Early automobiles were for recreation rather than transportation; their proud owners kept them in the barn on weekdays, using teams and buggies to get somewhere, bringing out their new contraptions on weekends when they would get them started and go out for a spin on Sunday afternoons. Wives accompanied their husbands, sometimes sitting in solitary splendor in the tonneau while their spouses wrestled with the mechanics of the machine in the front seat. Parades, dear to the heart of the upper-middleclass of the Edwardian era, were never complete without automobiles decorated with bunting or flowers for the occasion. Although most towns of any size in Nebraska had some paving of sorts by 1910 -- after all, Nebraska manufactured millions of paving bricks every year -- most of the streets were still deeply-rutted dirt roads which water-wagons sprinkled during the heat of summer to settle the dust.

Before long, steam cars and electrics lost out to internal combustion automobiles. And the motorcar changed. Carbide lamps were added, so that if a man got out and lit a match to the lamp he could drive at night. Cloth tops were added for protection from sun and rain, and windshields and even windows all the way around so that no longer did driver or passengers have to wear goggles. Cranks were a problem, to be sure, for careless drivers broke their arms when they forgot to hang loose to the crank which started the engine. After Henry Ford began putting out his Model T -- he manufactured fifteen million of them between 1909 and 1928 -- towns in Nebraska, as well as elsewhere, were a sea of black cloth-topped automobiles on Saturday nights, everybody driving to town to see and be seen in their fancy machines.

By 1920 there were so many automobiles in Nebraska, 205,000 of them, that the secretary of state in Lincoln could no longer handle their licensing. On December 10, 1921, counties began the job. Douglas county had the most cars, so its licenses carried the 1 designation; Lancaster was second, and number 2, Gage county was third; Custer county was fourth. Although rankings have changed, the numbers assigned to the ninety-three counties almost sixty years ago are still the ones carried on Nebraska license plates.

The automobile fever which started at the turn of the century continues. In Nebraska in 1978, there were 1,454,386 motor vehicles registered to a total population of 1,483,791, almost one automobile for every man, woman, and child in the state.

THE LINCOLN HIGHWAY IN 1917

Highways

Trouble was, with all those new automobiles in Nebraska in the early years of the 20th century, there were mighty few places to drive them. A few blocks in town, maybe, but not much else. It was inevitable, of course, that the proud owners of the new machines would organize clubs -- Americans do, you know -- and that the clubs would set up excursions. By 1910, the Hastings Automobile Club, for instance, went all the way to Harvard and back, fifty automobiles, in a single day, and later in the year to Holstein and Roseland and back. Other automobile clubs in the state were equally vigorous, members going from one town to another in caravan to boost each other out of deep ruts, push each other up steep grades.

The automobiles were ready. But the roads weren't. Although Nebraska legislatures of 1869, 1871, and 1873 had said that county section lines were to be public roads, those roads were really no more than trails, adequate for high-stepping horses and slow-moving wagons, but not good enough for automobiles which were capable of reaching speeds as high as 35 miles per hour. In 1909 total road mileage in Nebraska was 80,338, but seventy-seven counties reported no improved roads at all. Road repair was a township responsibility.

Out of the various automobile clubs came support for various highway associations. Most of them were akin to Chambers of Commerce, getting their support from towns which would be on their routes. The Good Roads Association, which met in May, 1911, was interested in stimulating a good road from Omaha to Denver, proposing that a book be put out telling about turns and grades, with pictures showing various identifying landmarks so that travelers could "easily follow the highway through the state without asking questions of anybody." Out of that organization came the O-L-D highway (for Omaha, Lincoln, Denver) which in 1920 became the D-L-D, for the 1,700-mile highway from Detroit to Denver; it is now known as US 6.

Before long the Lincoln Highway Association was established, with the Nebraska branch one of the most active in the country. The route was laid out from New York City to San Francisco, in Nebraska following the Oregon Trail and passing through fifteen counties, fifty-three towns. "No other state in the Union has so many miles of level road as the Lincoln Highway -- across our state," said a brochure from the Nebraska branch which solicited funds in 1914 for planting trees along the roadside. And the Lincoln Highway, which later became US 30, was a marvel of the age, for it had occasional concrete markers identifying the highway, far better than descriptions of turns at barns or cottonwood thickets which had been the only highway advice heretofore. Later on the Lincoln Highway Association secured from cement manufacturers an offer to supply free to any community three thousand barrels of cement if the town would see to improving a section of highway in its area; Grand Island, Kearney, and Fremont took advantage of the offer.

But although Nebraskans continued to buy automobiles at an astonishing rate, most of the taxpayers weren't interested in spending money on roads. It was the Federal Aid Road Act of 1916, providing federal funds to match state money, that was the impetus for early development of roads within the state, particularly for those highways which were part of an interstate road system. By 1921, 5,619 miles of Nebraska roads were included in the federal system, including one from Sioux City to Chadron (later called US 20), the Lincoln highway, the D-L-D, the one from Ogallala to Scottsbluff (later numbered US 26), the road from Sioux City to the Kansas line (later numbered US 77), and the one from Yankton through York to the Kansas line (later numbered US 81). Before the roads were numbered, they had names, even though the drivers couldn't ever be sure where to turn at a fork. These included the S-Y-A, for the Seward-York-Aurora route; The Harding, Columbia, Grainland, Potash; presumably drivers knew where they were and where they went.

By the early 1920's, some enterprising towns along highways set up touring facilities in city parks to attract motorists. There on bulletin boards they posted up-to-date information about road conditions ahead, including detours. For the fine new graveled roads almost always had road-graders somewhere along their lengths which were hazardous to pass on the narrow roadway; after the driver had

104

completed the maneuver he often found himself with a flat tire, the grader blade having kicked up glass or nails which caused punctures. The gravel pile in the center of the road was another peril, and loose gravel flipped many a car which had to brake to negotiate 90-degree turns on the highway.

In 1926 Nebraska highways were numbered and marked with metal signs, and gas stations which had sprouted up along the roadsides began to distribute free roadmaps. And other advertising evolved, itinerant painting crews wandering through the countryside offering to paint barns if the farmers would allow such slogans as "Carter's Little Liver Pills" or "Pink Pills for Pale People." A few years later, during the Depression years, drivers and passengers alike chuckled at the Burma-Shave signs which appeared in sequence along the highways, catchy limericks ending in an advertisement for shaving material.

Though Nebraska roads carried heavy traffic, they were far from adequate, far behind the standards of other states. By 1930, 5,000 miles were graveled, 3,300 more were graded, but only 309 miles were paved. Increased federal highway funding during the 1930's for work relief projects and in the years since has helped; with the opening of Interstate 80 and improvement of other roads within the state, Nebraska has begun to catch up.

Prairie Fires

Fed by tinder-dry native grass, fanned by high winds, prairie fires were the scourge of the Great Plains in the hot dry weeks of late summer and early fall. Whether they were set by embers from travelers' campfires in the days of the Overland Trail, or by sparks from tall-stacked wood-burning locomotives, or by lightning from a summer electrical storm, prairie fires were agents of destruction, sweeping across miles of plains, blistering infernos destroying everything in their path. In the ashes of the blackened earth after the blaze had died lay the hopes and dreams of early homesteaders, along with skeletons of animals caught in the flames and occasionally those of people as well.

Indians taught the early settlers not to try to outrun the blaze but to seek refuge on the nearest bare ground, either sand or dirt without grass, digging down if possible to escape the intense heat. Homesteaders later developed procedures to protect against fire, plowing furrows around buildings or hay stacks or growing fields, then plowing more furrows about twenty feet beyond; in the fall they fired the dry grass in-between, lighting the blaze on a still day with plenty of men around to control it with wet gunny-sacks. Later if a prairie fire

106

did fan out across the countryside, this charred area served as a fire-break, starving the oncoming wall of flame. It was a classic example of fighting fire with fire.

Possibly the worst prairie fire in Nebraska in terms of loss of life happened in October, 1873, when wind swept flames toward a country schoolhouse in Saline county. Against the teacher's objections, one of the mothers took some of the children and started home, trying to outrun the blaze. The blackened, scorched bodies of ten children and the mother were found later; those who had stayed with the teacher took refuge in a piece of bare ground and were saved. In Wayne county on October 18, 1879, Mrs. W. E. Durin took her daughter with her when she set out during a prairie fire to try to save a shed; she stumbled and fell, and "being large and clumsy, was caught by the fire," according to Andreas' *History of Nebraska*. Both were burned to death. And in Antelope county on July 14, 1874, Mrs. Henry Rogers died while helping the men fight a prairie fire; whether she was felled by the sun's heat or that of the prairie fire, nobody knew but she died nevertheless.

The autumn of 1872 was so dry that many prairie fires swept across Nebraska. In October a huge fire roared into Butler county from the west, swept south, then north, and south again, "singeing the entire county, the fiery tongue leaping over impossible spaces, jumping hedgerows one hundred feet in width, licking up in its unimpeded course hundreds of acres of standing corn, more than five thousand bushels of harvested wheat and other grains in granary.... implements...scores of cows, horses and pigs roasted alive," according to George L. Brown, writing later in *Nebraska History Magazine*. In October and November fire broke out in Adams and Clay counties so that "the country all around us for miles is black as ink," the Rev. Isaac Newell wrote to his wife back in Alton, Illinois. He described creating a firebreak and said "it seemed strange to stand upon a little piece of land of not more than four or five acres and see the fire rush on rapidly all around, seeming to devour everything in its tracks." On November 14, fire broke out from a dugout, burned a large area near Harvard, eventually crossing the railroad tracks and extending northward nearly to the Platte.

Some of the prairie fires were set deliberately. The most spectacular was that in October, 1864, set by the U.S. cavalry to control Indians. Soldiers put the torch to a four-hundred mile stretch from Fort Kearny to the Colorado line, utilizing the scorched-earth tactic that soldiers from Julius Caesar onward have known about; the flames stretched across southwest Nebraska into western Kansas and eastern Colorado and down to the Texas panhandle, where they finally died. Another one, in Hall county, was set as a grudge in 1859 by three men on their way home from the gold fields. Presumably annoyed at some settlers, they set a fire that swept over the whole settlement. In Frontier, Harlan and Furnas counties in October, 1873, political feelings ran so high that some politicians set a fire that kept people from going to the polls. High winds swept the flames from Prairie Dog Creek in the

107

south to the Platte river near Grand Island; men were so busy fighting the fire they could not leave to cast their votes in the general election that day.

Whole towns sometimes were threatened. In Grand Island a prairie fire caused by an ember from a passing train was fanned by a strong southwest wind and put the whole town in peril. In North Platte on April 7, 1893, a fire burned much of the town and surrounding countryside; a Mrs. Ogler, living south of town, went out to watch, misjudged the speed of the flames, and was burned to death; her two sons were badly burned trying to rescue her.

Even now, range fires are a hazard in rural Nebraska in the late summer and early fall. It is still possible for fires to start and be swept across vast reaches of dry grasslands.

The Farmer-Inventors

Early-day settlers discovered that farming in Nebraska, particularly in the central and western reaches of the state, called for far different procedures and equipment than anything they had known before, whether they came from eastern United States or Northern Europe. Although the soil was fertile, it was semi-arid, and the almost-constant wind further dried it. Whereas in other locations, they could rely on natural rainfall to make crops grow, in Nebraska they had to overcome the hot, dry, windy climate so that they could make use of the richness of the soil.

Even before the College of Agriculture was opened in 1882, university professors experimented with ideas for dry-land farming, and out in the state the farmers themselves began to work out methods of conserving soil moisture. For the most part they began with tools they had known before but they adapted and refined them for specific use on Nebraska farmland, a natural outgrowth of the make-do philosophy that has always flourished in the state.

When their neighbors discovered how effective these implements were, they wanted them too, and the farmer-tinkers began making them for others. Out of tinkers' sheds, blacksmiths' shops and small foundries evolved an industry, the

109

manufacturing of agricultural implements, now a five-hundred million dollar a year industry within Nebraska.

By 1880, the Nebraska Manufacturing Company in Lincoln was turning out harrows, hay rakes and windmills; Miles Lewis in Hastings was manufacturing grain headers; Calvin Bowman in Orleans, plows; Climax Windmill Factory in Falls City, windmills; the Columbus Foundry, well-boring equipment; and the Reed Plow Company in Nebraska City, plows, until its factory burned down in 1876. Dozens of other, smaller shops were also turning out farm equipment, perhaps several hundred units a year or only a dozen or so, all serving to help the new dryland farmers.

Before long, there were others. Charles Dempster in Beatrice quit selling windmills manufactured by others and started his own factory, eventually opening branches in Omaha, Oklahoma City, Denver, Kansas City, Sioux Falls and Amarillo, Texas, producing so many windmills that the Dempster logo was a familiar sight on the Great Plains farms. The Fairbury Windmill Company also produced windmills in large quantities. The Luebben Baler Company of Lincoln manufactured horse-drawn equipment which made cylindrical bales of hay and clover; Hall and Neiswanger of Cambridge, cultivators for listed corn.

Not all of the inventions made their creators wealthy. William F. Lillie invented the corn husker, or corn hook, an improvement on the old corn peg, but although it was produced in quantity and widely copied, he remained a relatively poor man.

In the 1900's, the M.M. Johnson Company of Clay Center began producing Old Trusty incubators, and developed an early-day radio station, KMMJ, to advertise its product. Hastings Equity Grain Bin Company of Hastings began manufacturing grain bins and water tanks for livestock in 1910; Miller Manufacturing in Grand Island, discs; Nebraska Engineering in Omaha, grain augers; Miller Manufacturing Company of Stratton, discs; and Miller Weeder Company, also of Stratton, rod weeders and flex chisels. Western Land Roller Company of Hastings started with the production of land-rollers and before long, expanded to manufacturing haying equipment, feed grinders, and eventually irrigation pumps.

Many early-day small-time manufacturers fell by the roadside and left no record of their accomplishments. Some of the men were better tinkers and inventors than they were businessmen. Others could not adjust to changes in agricultural procedures as farming became more and more mechanized; they kept on manufacturing buggy whips, as it were.

But others took their places, producing new kinds of equipment for Nebraska farmers in a changing age. Chief Industries of Grand Island, Behlen of Columbus, and others began to manufacture steel storage buildings. At the end of World War II, when farmers realized the importance of pump-irrigation, a new industry developed. The Valley Company purchased the patent which a Columbus inventor had for a center-pivot irrigation system, refined it and put it into production. Later

manufacturers of the self-propelled center-pivot systems which have revolution-
ized the Great Plains farming include the Reinke Company of Deshler, the Olson
Company of Atkinson, Lindsay Manufacturing Company of Lindsay, Lockwood of
Gering, and T and L of Hastings.

Many of the new agriculturally-related industries now export their products
around the world. Not only is Nebraska producing food for the world; she is also
sending the equipment so that others can produce food for themselves.

THE SAVIDGE BROTHERS AND THEIR PLANE

Aviation

The big sky of the Plains which filled the Indians with wonder seemed to appeal to the new white settlers in a different fashion: their young men wanted to conquer it. Neither group could imagine that in the latter half of the 20th century, the brilliant blue sky arching over Nebraska wheatfields would be criss-crossed with white man-made clouds, vapor trails marking the paths of machines carrying millions of people through the air at speeds far surpassing those of the fastest cranes or geese or hawks.

In the late summer of 1910, less than seven years after Wilbur and Orville Wright soared to fame at Kitty Hawk, the air age came to Nebraska. The first flimsy plane wobbled aloft in Omaha with Glenn H. Curtis at the primitive controls; six weeks later, at the 1910 State Fair in Lincoln, the first plane crashed in Nebraska. From then on would-be airmen tinkered in backyard sheds with wood and wires, poles and tubes, muslin, motors and bicycle tires, and before the year was out, a number had flown, among them Charles and Gus Baysdorfer of Omaha, whose plane was the first one made-in-Nebraska. The next year, after they finished building their third plane, they joined an aerial circus. In 1911, too, the Savidge brothers -- George, John, Joe, Dave, Phillip, Louis and Matt -- took their craft to the air near Ewing, a plane designed from ideas George contrived after he inadvertently sailed off a hayrack when he tried to take off a sheepskin coat during a high wind. Whichever brother piloted the Savidge plane sat in a seat unscrewed from a mowing machine. Eventually Matt became so skilled a pilot he became a skywriter, tracing his name in the sky and outlining it from smoke candles tied to the wings. The Savidges barnstormed over the country, thrilling gawking spectators. When Matt died in a crash in 1916, however, the family gave up flying. A Historical Land Mark Council was dedicated in 1968 near Ewing to commemorate the Savidge brothers' efforts.

Another early-day flyer was Jimmie Ward, who transported his "Shooting Star" by train, stopping at various communities to screw it together, while the town band and sometimes a drill team stirred up an enthusiastic audience. He took off at speeds of thirty-five miles an hour and sailed into the air, sometimes as high as 3,500 feet, maybe even 5,000, depending on the winds, dipping and gliding and spiraling, and then landing on his bicycle wheels. The Adams County Historical Society has erected a marker on the Hastings College campus indicating Jimmie Ward's flights there on July 17-18, 1911.

In 1915 Nebraska became the first state to have its own National Guard Air Force, two bi-planes, one owned by D.W. Schaffer and the other by Ralph W. McMillen, with two other pilot-mechanics as support staff. Since there was no funding, state or federal, the air force financed its existence through exhibition flights at county fairs. A few months later when Captain Schaffer's plane crashed, the air force strength was cut in half, but Captain McMillen kept on flying, made simulated bombings of the penitentiary and down-town Lincoln, flying as far as Omaha one October day, his only difficulty a slight collision with an automobile as he landed there to deliver some letters and a shirt a man had forgotten to pick up at a Lincoln laundry. The next year he practiced night bombing over Lincoln, inadvertently hitting a streetcar. But when Nebraska National Guard units were sent to the Mexican border in 1916, the War Department neglected to include the air force.

When the United States went into World War I, young Nebraskans flocked to join the new U.S. Air Corps to fight the Huns, the Red Baron in mid-air. Fort Omaha became a balloon school. At the end of the war Ray and Ethel Page in Lincoln began converting surplus army planes for peacetime use, established the Nebraska Standard Corporation at 2409 O, and manufactured other planes. Other factories started so that by 1922 Lincoln was recognized as the third largest aircraft manufacturing center in the United States. E.J. Sias was the founder of the Lincoln Flying School. The 1920's were the hey-day for hundreds of mustered-out army pilots and newly-taught ones who barnstormed across the Plains performing acrobatics, wingwalking, other feats of aeronautical wizardry for admiring audiences ringing the pasture below.

One of the students in 1922 at Page Field at 20th and Calvert was a young Swede from Minnesota, Charles Augustus Lindbergh, whose teachers were Ira Biffle, E.G. Ball, E.B. Barnes and Aaron Ball. On May 21, 1927, he achieved immortality by becoming the first person to fly the Atlantic alone. He was celebrated as the Lone Eagle, feted around the world. Three months later he flew over Nebraska, an official flight in his "Spirit of St. Louis" plane, circling Lincoln, Columbus, Hastings, Kearney, Lexington, McCook, Imperial, and Bird City, Kansas, on his 7½-hour flight from Omaha to Denver. Thousands of persons rushed out-of-doors to wave at him.

A year later the first air mail left Lincoln. On July 9, 1928, a plane piloted by a former University of Nebraska student, R.L. "Rube" Wagner, took off for the east, leaving several hundred sweaty spectators in the dust of the prop-wash. The plane carried 20,000 pieces of mail and two passengers, Sam Waugh and R.E. Campbell, first passengers on a scheduled flight out of Lincoln.

In the years since, almost every town of any size in Nebraska has developed some sort of airfield; farmers, ranchers, professional people, corporations have planes, and commercial lines have been established. During World War II army air bases operated at Alliance, Ainsworth, Bruning, Fairmont, Grand Island, Harvard, Kearney, Lincoln, McCook, Scottsbluff and Scribner. Airplanes are now used as ambulances, for traffic control, to tow advertising streamers over the University of Nebraska stadium, and for a variety of other purposes.

FRANCIS SCORES FIRST TOUCHDOWN FOR THE HUSKERS IN THE ROSE BOWL GAME

Go Big Red

It isn't viral, it isn't bacterial. But it is highly contagious. It's Scarlet Fever, the Go Big Red Disease that affects Nebraskans every fall, particularly on glorious Saturday afternoons when the sky is clear incredible blue, the sunlight golden, and the air crisp and invigorating. Then the afflicted converge upon the stadium in Lincoln, tens of thousands of red-clad human beings who brave ticket scalpers, highway troopers, food purveyors and parking lot operators to get there. On football Saturdays, the nearly 80,000 feverish spectators in the stadium comprise the third largest city in Nebraska.

But the disease isn't confined simply to the stadium. Elsewhere in Lincoln, and outstate as well, so many other persons are affected by it that business and industry screech to a halt, for most of the state seems glued to the radio to hear what's going on in Memorial Stadium.

It all started in 1890 when the University of Nebraska administration timidly allowed Ebenezer Mockett and some friends to play a football game. For seven years students had urged that the sport be adopted; after all, Ivy League colleges had it, and even Doane and Hastings Colleges right here in Nebraska. Dr. Langdon Frothingham coached the dozen players who straggled through that year's two-game schedule: Omaha YMCA, when five hundred students went along to watch; and Doane, that game played in February. The next year there was no coach for the three games the team played against Doane, but for the fourth game, against Iowa, the Iowa coach helped the fledgling Nebraska team. In 1892 the University hired a coach, Frank Campbell, who struggled to find teams for matches; for several years the Nebraskans played any teams they could find: the Omaha, Denver and Sioux City Athletic Clubs, the Kansas City Medics, and Baker, Grinnell, Ottawa, Tarkio, Bellevue, Wesleyan, Hastings and William Jewell Colleges -- even Lincoln High School among others.

Although the rules were flexible and the schedules spasmodic, there was enthusiasm on campus for the team which was so sophisticated the players had matching stockings and somewhat similar uniforms; on some other teams players wore football suits stitched up at home of varying colors, patterns and materials. Engineering students had laid out the playing field; Roscoe Pound served as umpire for half of one game; Willa Cather and Dorothy Canfield wrote a football story for the campus newspaper.

In the 1890's, the universities of Nebraska, Iowa, Kansas and Missouri formed a western Collegiate Football Association, the first of what were to be a number of successive conferences, and began drafting primitive eligibility rules; in years past, outsiders were sometimes encouraged to play, in one game the Nebraska coach himself had played.

It was a Lincoln *Star* sports writer, C.S. (Cy) Sherman who named the team in 1900; until then they had been called the Rattlesnakes, Antelopes or Bug Eaters. In his column he called them the Cornhuskers, and the name stuck.

Year by year, as traditions evolved, football enthusiasm mounted in Nebraska, fed by Coach E.O. (Jumbo) Stiehm's Stiehm Rollers of the mid-1910's, winning years of the golden 1920's, astonishing performances by Johnny Bender, Guy Chamberlin, Ed Weir, others. In 1923 Memorial Stadium was dedicated to the memory of World War I soldiers; at the last game at the old field, south of the new one, 15,000 people had jammed in to watch Nebraska trounce Notre Dame, so the need for new facilities was obvious.

And the faithful followed the teams to the other states; as early as 1901, twenty-five hundred Nebraskans went to Minneapolis by train to cheer their favorites against a formidable foe; later they would go by automobile, chartered bus, then plane, even to such far-away places as Pasadena and Miami and Hawaii, to the delight of restaurateurs and hoteliers who could count on balancing their budgets in a Nebraska year.

Cheerleaders, bands, Joyce Ayres and Wilbur Chenoweth's "Hail Varsity" and other specially-written Nebraska songs, raccoon coats, felt pennants, the card section flipping designs in the student part of the stands -- football Saturday was electric with excitement. Not even the Depression of the early 1930's could dis-

116

courage Cornhusker supporters, for those years coincided with Dana X. Bible's eight seasons of victories. His players included the phenomenal George Sauer, Bernie Masterson, Clair Bishop and Bruce Kilbourne, teammates from Lincoln High games who went onto the university field together and never lost a game in Lincoln. The marching band was well-established, and in 1939 Director Don Lentz inaugurated Band Day, first in the nation, with thousands of high school musicians performing at half-time on the field. Later came the Golden Girl, a baton twirler.

After Bible came Coach Biff Jones, and such players as Lloyd Cardwell and Sam Francis. And the Rose Bowl of 1940, the date that for some Nebraskans measures the beginning of the world. "I lived in Nebraska three years before I found out Nebraska lost in the Rose Bowl," someone said later, according to James Denney, Howard Silber and Hollis Limprecht in the book, *Go Big Red*. Just to go was enough. But the late 1940's and 1950's were lack-lustre days when only truly dedicated Nebraskans had the time to watch more defeats than victories on the field. There were occasional flashes of brilliance, to be sure -- Tom Novak, Bobby Reynolds -- but there were empty seats in the stadium.

The magnificent days lay just ahead, for Bob Devaney became coach in 1962 and in his eleven years and Tom Osborne's going-on seven, the Cornhuskers have reached pinnacles of football glory: Number One rating in the country, bowl games almost every year, a chain of astonishing victories. Johnny Rodgers and the Heisman award; Larry Jacobson and Rich Glover and the Outland award; All-American players. Oklahoma has replaced Minnesota as the Foe. The several-times-enlarged stadium jammed with red-clad spectators -- some of them 'tis said, red from the skin out, to their red coats and red shoes -- isn't big enough; season tickets figure in bequests, in divorce settlements. Dedicated Huskers salt their food from Big Red shakers, read by light from Big Red lamps, toot their "There Is No Place Like Nebraska" horns on their vans. Football has become a way of life.

Little did Ebenezer Moffett realize back in 1890 that he would instill such patriotic fervor, such pride, in Nebraska, that Go Big Red would be the rallying cry for the whole state!

117

FARMER HUSKING CORN

Corn Husking

In the fall when the air is crisp with the chill of the first frost, farmers a generation or two ago in Nebraska checked the corn hanging from the stalks in the field, found the yellow kernels hard and dented, or dimpled, and ready for harvest. It was time for cornhusking. They readied their gear for the solitary job that lay ahead, one of hard physical labor. Unlike the harvesting of wheat, which was a group activity involving a number of men working together, cornhusking was generally a lonesome chore, a man working alone in the field or perhaps with a half-grown son to help him. Only at cornhusking bees, which were special, was there sociability.

The farmer located his husking glove and peg, and went out to rig the bangboard onto the wagon, adding a couple of planks to one side of the wagon to make it higher than the other. Then he hitched his team to the wagon and headed toward the field. While the team plodded through the cornfield, the wagon straddling a row of corn, the cornhusker picked the corn, stalk after stalk, using the curved husking knife or peg strapped to the palm of the heavy husking glove to slash off the dried husk around the ear of corn. Then he twisted the ear free of

118

the stalk and tossed it into the wagon, hitting the bangboard so that the ear fell neatly into the wagon bed below. Each movement was so deft and so controlled that a good workman working steadily and rhythmically could pick as much as seventy or eighty bushels in a single day, if the stalks were tall, close together, with good ears on them.

There was a regular movement to the procedure, and even the team was caught up in it; from long years of practice the horses could tell from the thumps how fast to move through the field to keep pace with the man. The sounds fitted the almost ballet-like aura of rhythmic motions: the rustle of the dried stalks and leaves as the man and equipment brushed against them, the rasping as the man ripped off the husk, the snapping as he tore the cob from the stalk, the thud as the cobs fell into the wagon-bed, and from time to time the man's chucking noises to the team, whether to slow it down, speed it up, or merely acknowledge its presence there in the expanse of rattling leaves.

In dry years, when the stalks were sparse and short, the farmer could not work as fast nor as efficiently. He sometimes got kinks in his back from having to lean over to reach the cob, and sometimes it was a walk, rather than a step, to the next stalk. Those years, twenty or thirty bushels of corn meant a good day's work.

When the wagon bed was full of ears of corn, the farmer drove the wagon back to the farmyard to unload the corn into the corncrib, a circular enclosure made of wired slats which allowed air to circulate to finish the drying process for the kernels. As the corn was needed for feed it was shelled, at first by a hand-cranked apparatus, later by a powered one. The hard kernels went to the live-stock, the corn-cobs to the kitchen to fuel the cookstove.

No matter the number of acres a man had in corn, the thrifty farmer had his cornhusking finished by Thanksgiving, his cribs full. Only the shiftless one would have lolligagged around so he was still in the cornfield after the last of November, unless it was a wet fall or an early snowy winter.

But when a man was down -- sick, injured, unable to work -- or if a new widow had no sons to bring in the corn, the neighborhood gathered together for a husking bee, farmers bringing their teams, wagons, and husking gloves to do the job for their neighbor, contributing their services, not knowing when they themselves might need a helping hand. A neighborhood husking bee was not only philanthropic; it was also a sociable occasion. Whole families came, the women with bowls or platters of food wrapped in clean tea-towels for a communal dinner at noon-day. A husking bee provided women a rare occasion to be with their neighbors, to talk to other women as they worked together, discussing recipes, quilt patterns, household remedies and other womanly topics. The youngsters found playmates there to play tag with, or help locate the new kittens in the barn, or else peer at from the shelter of mother's skirts.

In the 1920's and 1930's, under the aegis of the county extension services, cornhusking contests developed on county, state and national levels. On a given

119

day in early November, entrants gathered at a farm where corn rows of uniform length had been marked off, and at a signal, the contestants started off, one to a row, husking, twisting, flinging their ears of corn into the waiting wagons. The first man through was usually declared the winner if his ears were cleanly husked, but he was disqualified if he left too much husk. Not only did county winners have the satisfaction of knowing they were the best in the area and eligible to go on to the state contest, but they also won cash prizes contributed by local banks and businessmen. State winners had even larger prizes, and the national winners were celebrated indeed. For many years the *Nebraska Farmer* magazine sponsored the national contest, and in 1933, Sherman Henrikson of Lancaster county was the national champion, husking an astonishing 27.62 bushels of corn in thirty minutes at a farm near West Point.

With the use of mechanical corn pickers in the years since World War II, cornhusking has become faster, more efficient, and less colorful. Although there is skill in the way the farmer operates his machine, the challenge is different: cornhusking no longer is a matter of brawn, coordination and rhythm. It is mechanical. National cornpicking contests are still held, usually under the sponsorship of implement companies. One was held in Grand Island several years ago.

SVOBODA & GARBER BRICKYARD IN ST. PAUL, 1899

Brickmaking

Bricks, tons of them, millions of them. Bricks for buildings, bricks for sidewalks, bricks for paving. Bricks of many colors. All of them from Nebraska.

In the first frenzied construction after Nebraska was opened for settlement, buildings were made of rough-hewn boards hammered together in haste. With commercial areas built of incendiary-type material, with recurring prairie fires swooping across the plains and with sparks thrown out of the tall smokestacks of the frequent trains, and with only primitive hand-powered fire-combatting equipment, fires were commonplace, sections of almost every village going up in smoke with monotonous regularity. By the 1880's town fathers decreed that from then on commercial construction would be of fire-retardant materials. But where would they come from? The only stone quarry of any size, near Beatrice, produced only limestone; bricks were so heavy that freight charges made them prohibitively expensive when they were shipped in. There had to be some solution to the problem of finding adequate fireproof building materials.

And there was, close at hand. From the ground, homesteaders created sod-houses -- and from the ground, others found clay of such good quality that it could be used for brickmaking. The answer lay under foot, with no freight charges. Before long there were brickyards operating in Lincoln, Hastings, Beatrice, Calhoun, Nelson, Nebraska City, Omaha, Sutton, Fremont, Juniata, Roseland, other areas. In Adams county in 1886 a whole community call Brickton was planned around a clay pit; when the company ran into financial difficulties after the burst of the Boom of 1886 the village didn't develop although for years the area was still called Brickton. Some of the brickyards were small, operating only for a few years and supplying bricks only for the immediate neighborhood; others were enormous, producing quantities of bricks.

Using techniques developed centuries earlier, brickmakers scraped clay from the ground, took it to horse-powered grinders which pulverized it, and then added enough water to make a paste which they rolled out in a thick ribbon and cut by hand into bricks. Crews set the wet bricks to dry in the air, and days later put them into huge coal-fired kilns where they baked at high temperatures for several days and cooled almost as long. The pattern on the brick-face was determined by the die on the extruder as the paste came out, and the color by the clay itself and the length and intensity of the firing.

Towns replaced their wooden sidewalks with brick ones, paved dusty rutted streets with brick. The demand for brick was astronomical. For thirty years Hastings was a brickmaking center, supplying all the paving brick for the state and some for other uses, its four yards producing upwards of fifty million brick a year. Yankee Hill in Lincoln, and later Endicott Brick and Tile Company, were other large-scale manufacturers, specializing in face brick shipped to sites all over the country. In the Hastings yards, much of the work in the labor-intensive industry was provided by Germans from Russia, in Lincoln by Irish and Czechs.

In time other construction materials evolved, particularly for streets and sidewalks, and demand for brick lessened. By that time many of the clay beds were exhausted and the factories so in need of mechanization that many of the brickyards in the state closed, marginal ones early, others about the time of World War II. The ones that were left became larger, more efficient. Yankee Hill in Lincoln, in constant operation since 1881, produces about twenty million face brick a year from native clay. Endicott Brick and Tile, near Fairbury, in operation intermittently from 1920 onward, continuously since 1950, produces fifty million brick a year, some of it face brick, some of it paving and sidewalk brick, some of it ceramic tile, in a highly mechanized plant. The Los Angeles area is its biggest market.

Other building material than bricks also began to come from the soil. In Jefferson county it was lime from the white rock quarried there, used as a mortar and also as a whitewash. As early as 1848, U.S. soldiers produced it, and the earliest settlers in the 1860's burned it themselves in primitive ovens. In 1876 the first commercial kiln was built and for the next twenty years was in production, burning the native rock to reduce it to a powder. The Jefferson County Historical Society has preserved a kiln as a historic site.

In Superior the ground provided material for cement. The original company began in 1911, operated intermittently for a few years, and in 1917 the plant was taken over by the Ideal Cement Company which has produced Portland cement ever since. The limestone and clay which are the raw materials come from nearby quarries, hauled on the company's own railway, and in slurry form are fired in kilns at 2800 degree temperatures. The chemical changes created by the intense heat produce Portland cement, a powdery substance so greatly in demand for all kinds of construction -- highways, buildings -- that the Superior plant is in operation twenty-four hours a day, producing more than 250,000 tons of Portland cement each year.

From the ground they stood on, Nebraskans have been able to create building materials, not only for themselves but for the use of others throughout the country.

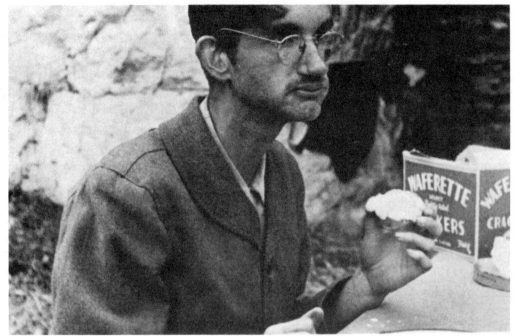

The Great Depression

Even though for the rest of the country the Great Depression took place in the 1930's, following the crash on Wall Street in 1929, for many Nebraskans, particularly farmers, it really began in the 1920's.

The high prices for wheat during World War I had encouraged many of them to mortgage what they had to buy more land, more equipment, so that they could grow more wheat for more money. Mortgage debt on Nebraska farms increased 170 percent during the period from 1910 to 1920. But when the price of wheat plummeted in the 1920's, so did the farmers' fortunes, for they were saddled with trying to pay high-interest mortgages with low-interest produce. As a result, many of them lost their farms during the 1920's, and in a sort of domino effect, the country banks which had made the mortgages also failed, six hundred fifty Nebraska banks closing their doors during the 1920's.

As farmers were forced to leave their farms, businesses in small towns were affected, for they were dependent on farmers for their existence. The precarious financial situation of the farmers came at a time when villages were beginning to decline in population and economic significance anyhow, for the beginning of

124

the automobile age had started customers to drift toward larger towns for their marketing needs. While the rest of the country seemed to be busy with the Charleston, bootleg gin, automobiles and radios and all the other symbols of the Jazz Age, Nebraska farmers and farming communities were ailing. The stock market crash in 1929 which caused businesses all over the country to go into a tailspin simply added to the economic problems that already plagued Nebraska.

In the early 1930's the jobless from other parts of the country began to move through Nebraska, men riding the rails, hopping freight trains to move from town to town seeking work, some riding inside an empty freight car, others on top or hanging to the undercarriage. It was a rare freight train in those days that did not have unofficial passengers hanging on it as it chugged across the countryside. Once in town the men asked for work, and finding none, went from house to house knocking on doors to ask housewives for food, a hand-out, many of them offering to rake leaves, fix roofs, or do other odd-jobs in return for a meal. Although housewives rarely invited them into the house, most of them did hand plates of food out the back door, sharing what they had with those less fortunate. Part of it was the time-honored prairie custom of helping those in need, and part of it may have been a feeling that there but for the grace of God go I.

Towns and charitable organizations did what they could to help, setting up buildings as dormitories where itinerants could sleep, supplying them with meal tickets for the bread-line at the Salvation Army, Red Cross, or wherever the hungry were fed rations of bread, bologna, cheese and coffee. Restaurants turned over their excess food at the end of the day to the feeding stations. For the most part, everyone felt compassion for the people who were down-and-out mostly through no fault of their own. A reporter on the Hastings *Spotlight* termed the sleeping quarters for itinerants in his town the Hoosegow Hotel for they were housed in the old jail.

Eventually, though, it was not just itinerants who were hungry but neighbors. Businesses folded, townspeople were out of work. Those who had jobs found their wages or salaries cut. Teachers in Omaha, other areas, were paid in warrants or promissory notes, for tax receipts were so low there wasn't enough money in the till to pay them.

Church groups, civic clubs such as Kiwanis and Rotary, and other organizations tried to help, eventually banding together in county relief committees to dispense food, groceries, blankets, shoes to local persons in need. One teacher recalls suggesting to a listless child in her class that she go home to rest and eat, only to be told that "Oh, no, today is my sister's turn to eat!" Another woman remembers that for a period of a month, the only food her family of seven had was a case of canned split pea soup somebody gave them.

To clothe their families, mothers made underwear of flour sacks, remade grown-up clothing to fit youngsters, sewed garments out of curtains. Fathers resoled shoes with rubber from discarded automobile tires. Families doubled up, married children and their youngsters moving back home to their parents, sometimes leaving their own homes after dark because they owed back rent. Enterprising young men whose idea of a fling was going to town on Saturday night knew to the drop how much water they could add to the short ration of gas in the automobile tank to stretch it.

In the absence of cash, people bartered, paying the doctor, the minister, with chickens, cream. One young lawyer survived because a client, a restaurant owner, swapped his legal fee for a meal ticket at the cafe. A small-town merchant remembers trading a winter coat for a jar of bootleg liquor. In some communities women's clubs held Women's Markets where town and country women could bring home-made jellies, canned fruit, dressed chickens, handwork of all kinds, to sell for cash.

Farm prices were at their lowest ebb: eggs were a nickel a dozen, milk a dime a gallon. In 1933 indignant farmers overturned milk-trucks on the highway near Omaha to protest low prices -- too bad, some people thought, when other people were starving. Later in the year farmers marched on the splendid brand-new capital building in Lincoln to urge a moratorium on farm debt. Wheat was 27 cents a bushel, corn 13 cents; a man couldn't make a living from that.

The Depression days of the early 1930's were desperate ones. But whereas the rest of the country began to recover by 1934, even worse days lay ahead for Nebraska and the Great Plains generally. Heat, drought, high winds -- the Dust Bowl was about to blow in, and at its height many farmers harvested so little corn or wheat the price was immaterial. The grimmest days lay just ahead.

THE APPROACH OF A DUST STORM

The Dust Bowl

In Nebraska's farm-oriented culture, land is the one sure card in the gambler's deck. The rain this year may be too little or too late, or the heat so intense it dries the crops in the field, or disease and pests rampant in the fields. But next year the good fertile earth will produce. If a man has land, he will do well: this conviction has provided continual optimism to the Nebraska farmer, one of the world's biggest gamblers.

But for three years of horror in the middle 1930's, when heat and drought had already tested the farmer's faith, the land itself was imperiled. It blew away. The topsoil swirled in thick gritty clouds that made a darkness at noon.

The Depression had belonged to America, and by 1934 America was beginning to recover. The Dust Bowl belonged to the Great Plains, and it blew in on a still-weak economy. Nebraska was not as hard hit by it as were parts of Kansas, Oklahoma and the Dakotas, but even so, the Dust Bowl had a profound effect upon the state, physically, economically and psychologically, especially in the southwestern reaches where it was the most severe.

127

Although the immediate cause of the Dust Bowl was a quirk of nature which brought high winds to land that had been pulverized by three years of drought and the driest summer in fifty-seven years, some of the cause was man-made, dating back to the time of World War I. Then farmers eager to cash in on two-dollar wheat broke the native sod in fragile areas, cultivating land that was too light to stand up to row-cropping and constant plowing. In times of adequate rainfall, the cultivated soil stayed in place; at other times of the cyclical climate pattern, when there was no root structure to hold it in place, the delicate soil blew away, eroding increasing amounts of land with each gust of wind.

The winds began in the spring of 1934, and they blew intermittently for the next three years, particularly in the spring, sweeping across the barren fields, whipping up clouds of dust. The sky turned murky, and from the southwest a churning cloud of dust rolled across the prairie, blotting out the sun, engulfing everything in its way. Persons caught in it could not see, could not breathe. When the wind finally died down, fine gritty dust lay over everything, piled up in drifts against fence posts and buildings, sifted under door frames and window sills, covering dishes in the cupboards, linens and clothing in closets, bathtubs, even babies in their cribs. Black blizzards, they were called, but when there was light again, it turned out that the grit sometimes had tinges of color to it -- a reddish cast, from Oklahoma soil, or a dirty yellow, or a plain dun color, depending on what part of the southwest had been churning that day.

So strong were the winds, so heavy the dust, that on occasion cities as far away as Chicago and beyond were affected.

When the winds died down the dust did not blow but the heat was always there in the summer months, days and weeks of temperatures well above one hundred degrees, stifling, inescapable heat in the pre-air-conditioning age. For relief, persons slept outdoors, on porches, in parks, sometimes waking up to find themselves covered with a fine sifting of dust that had settled during the night.

Combined with the heat was the drought, less than half the normal rainfall. Although during the Dust Bowl years there were occasional rains, they seemed to be either showers, when raindrops mixed with dust as they fell to create falling mud, or else gully-washers. Heavy rains in May, 1935, resulted in the flooding of the Republican river, bringing death to more than one hundred persons.

Despite the difficulties, people tried to go about their everyday business, farmers plowing and planting in the spring, sometimes only to see their land and seed sail off in the first dust storm. When fields germinated, they were sparse; when they grew, their yield was pitiful. Some years all the corn harvested from a quarter-section would fill only a couple of bushel baskets.

Two unusual physical ailments were associated with the dust: dust pneumonia, despite masks some people wore to filter out the dust that always seemed to be in the air; and a high incidence of ruptured appendixes. In the pre-penicillin age, country doctors evolved an innovative treatment to treat the usually-fatal problem;

128

rather than removing the appendix they inserted drains so the infection could dribble out, and their rate of recovery was phenomenal. Pneumonia also was responsible for the heavy livestock loss; starving cattle grubbing whatever green was in the pastures -- tumbleweeds, usually -- often rooted below the surface of the soft powdery soil and inhaled enough dirt to cause pneumonia. But such was their condition that they would have died of starvation anyhow in the dried-up pastures.

In 1936, a new element was added to the dust, drought and heat: an infestation of grasshoppers which stripped bark off trees, fruit off trees, leaves from whatever was green and growing. Poisons supplied by the federal government seemed to nourish them; the next year the grasshoppers were even worse.

Although there were still dust storms in 1937 and 1938, they abated in intensity and occurrence. The grasshoppers eventually died, the rains came back, and the summer heat was not so strong. By 1939 Nebraska was on its way out of the Depression, having survived the Dust Bowl.

But when the census takers came in 1940 to count the people in Nebraska, they learned that 65,000 had left the state in the ten years of the 1930's. They had gone West to get jobs, driven away by the mortgage, the heat, the drought, and most of all, by the dust.

MRS. WILLIAM LEE OF FALLS CITY PLAYING TUNES

Simple Pleasures, 1930's Style

In the depths of the Great Depression of the 1930's and the grimmer Dust Bowl years that followed, Nebraskans showed remarkable resiliency. Although at times they may not have known where the next meal was coming from, most of them retained their sense of humor, found pleasure in simple entertainment, and had a sense of identity with their fellow man. Few of them had money; those who did found it expedient to keep quiet, merging into the general pattern of economizing, making do, living cheap.

Friday night was free movie night in dozens of small villages, the social event of an otherwise dull week. Town merchants -- owners of the grocery, filling station, implement shop and general store, perhaps -- pooled their resources, rented movies, and during the summer months showed them in a vacant lot. During the day half-grown boys set up the seats -- planks and concrete blocks, usually stored in an empty building -- but some people brought their own chairs or else dragged the back seats from their Fords or Chevys over to the lot. The screen was the wall of a building; in Trumbull, for instance, it was the abandoned harness shop. In the hour between dusk and the start of the movie, hopefully the audience

130

would buy something in the local stores, keeping the money at home; some children of affluence even had ice cream cones from the drugstore every week, lapping at the drippings just as Tom Mix came onto the screen. Although the movie was silent, the audience was not, expressing its approval with whistles and shouts, its disapproval with hisses as Hoot Gibson, William S. Hart, Ken Maynard, Jack Holt, Thomas Meighan flashed across the brick wall of the prairie village. It was entertainment, and it was free.

Larger towns, those whose movie emporiums had been able to afford the transition to sound movies, and had survived, created such attractive merchandising gimmicks that going-to-the-movies became almost a ritual, families saving all week long to afford one or two twenty-five cent tickets each Saturday night. At first it was called Bank Nite: cash prizes were given persons in the theater whose names were called. But in 1937 the Nebraska Supreme Court outlawed the giving away of money, so theaters began giving away free things: dishes, silverware, pots-and-pans, anything they reckoned would draw crowds, some of them now collectors' items. The give-aways and the coolness of the building -- in many communities the only air-conditioning in town was in the water-cooled theater -- kept the places packed during the 1930's, not only on Bank Nite but on other days as well. Theaters showed movies continuously from 1 p.m. onward each day. The matinee price was a dime; evening theater-goers hurried to get there before 6:30 when the price went up to a quarter. Watching the predictable plots, the good-will-conquer-all stories, audiences could escape the humdrum, sometimes panicky situations of their own lives, forgetting the grimness of their existence as they watched Norma Shearer, Joan Crawford, Claudette Colbert and others emote on the Silver Screen. Movie magazines, by the way, were five or ten cents; *Colliers,* the *Saturday Evening Post* and *Liberty* were also a nickel, but the *American Magazine* cost more.

A few Nebraska communities had dance marathons, sponsored by promoters in local dance halls. The last surviving couple staggering around the floor, exhausted and footsore, won a cash prize. Some towns forbade the marathons on humanitarian grounds. Tom Thumb golf afforded would-be golfers a place to putt when they could not afford country club fees; the miniature course was better than none.

But there were some who could not afford even these simple pleasures. For them there were other forms of entertainment. Watching the streamliner come in was a favorite for those who lived near the Burlington or Union Pacific tracks. Nebraskans lined the rails to see the Denver Zephyr streak across the Burlington line in May, 1934, setting a world record of 77½ miles per hour on the Denver-to-Chicago run, and for years after that many of them enjoyed just going to the station to see who got off, who got on, finding vicarious pleasure in the bustle and excitement at the depot.

131

Jig-saw puzzles with thousands of pieces set up on the card table in the front room occupied hours of time; those who could not afford to buy puzzles from the dime store made their own, gluing a picture onto cardboard or plywood and sawing out the tiny pieces. That crossword puzzles achieved their greatest popularity during that time is evident still, for many of the clues in contemporary puzzles are geared to persons who were living during the 1930's. Contract bridge had replaced auction bridge or whist and provided free entertainment at home; other card games -- authors, touring, rook, pitch, pinochle and rummy -- were equally popular.

For the athletically-inclined, particularly the young, there was roller-skating, not in rinks but on sidewalks or paved city streets. A skate-key on a string worn around the neck was a status symbol; youngsters in families with many children and only one pair of skates took turns wearing the key to school. Several communities had Outdoor Clubs composed of young couples who walked on weekends, not for the sake of their pulse-rates but because walking afforded them a means of sociability and being out-of-doors, going to interesting sites within a fifteen mile radius or so of the town; it was cheaper than owning a car.

There were community events as well, musical productions, theatricals, others calling for the talents of volunteers. In much of Nebraska during the 1930's there seemed to be a high degree of cultural appreciation and participation.

The pleasures were simple, to be sure, but they were enough. No matter the poverty of the pocket. Even during the most trying years, Nebraskans possessed the imagination to create satisfying activities for their leisure hours.

WPA: REMOVING STREET CAR TRACK IN LINCOLN

Farmsteads and Other Alphabet Soup

One of the most intriguing but least-known footnotes to the Dust Bowl days in Nebraska was the Farmstead Program, a cooperative farming operation set up by the federal government to give a new chance to farmers between the ages of 21 and 50 who had lost their farms to mortgages and high winds. The program didn't last long; perhaps the idea was ahead of its time, for Congress cancelled it in its second or third year of operation. But while it lasted it was an interesting experiment in the conservation of people and of land.

Under the aegis of the Resettlement Administration one hundred twenty-nine families, apparently chosen by community leaders for their industriousness, were settled in eight locations in Nebraska -- Two Rivers, between the Platte and the Elkhorn; Falls City; Fairbury; Grand Island; Loup City; Kearney, South Sioux City; and Scottsbluff. Each family was assigned a four-acre plot for its own use and farmed cooperatively the rest of the land, sharing costs, labor and profits, paying back to the federal government with the interest the funds advanced for the land and for the building of the new homes and farm structures on the site. The families agreed to work under the guidance of the farm managers and home economists in soil conservation practices and nutritional service. But it scarcely got going before it was stopped. Contemporaries who knew the program and some of the participants then reported that the project seemed to be going well when, as often happens with governmental activities, it was cancelled, the land and buildings sold, and the people left to their own devices.

Other federal programs of the time were less innovative and many of them functioned for several years.

Federal help was not new to Nebraskans; even before Nebraska became a state its people sought it -- the Homestead Act and its various amendments -- and later in Smith-Hughes courses, highway funding, others. The magnitude of the Depression was such that local or state bodies could not cope with it, and when the Dust Bowl catastrophe swept across the Great Plains, drastic measures were called for to save human life and the land itself. The 1930's saw the beginning of the federal alphabet agencies, the first few under President Hoover and hundreds more under President Roosevelt. Now there are thousands.

The first need was to help people survive. After 1933, federal relief was provided not by alms or a direct dole but through work projects in which participants worked at productive labor to earn their subsistence. The CWA, PWA, CCC, and most of all, the WPA, sprang into existence, and towns all over Nebraska were hard put to it to think up jobs for the jobless. In fact, Governor Charley Bryan nearly lost out on funds for the state because Nebraska communities had never been very good at thinking big insofar as their needs were concerned. But before long, parks were cleaned up, privies rebuilt, brick pavements relaid, sewer lines built, bridges and overpasses and streets constructed, public buildings erected, all manner of improvements made. Most of the WPA projects were funded as joint ventures with the federal government, local governments providing a portion of the money; some of the projects, it turned out, were those that towns had earlier turned down as too expensive but when a little outside money was offered, they could do it. Sure, some people said, those WPA-ers don't work very fast; some of them just lean on their rakes. Even so, though, getting some work out of them is better than simply giving them food. Later on, out-of-work teachers, writers, and artists were assigned WPA work, teaching adult classes, writing histories, painting murals in public buildings.

The PWA funds were for such huge projects as the Tri-County dam near Ogallala and the Sherman dam on the Loup river. The Civilian Conservation Corps was composed of young men assigned to prune brush, clean out streams, prevent erosion on public lands; among sixteen camps in Nebraska were those at Beatrice and Chadron.

The second need was to help farmers, and dozens of agricultural alphabet agencies sprang up, many of them still functioning. The Farm Credit Administration consolidated all agricultural credit agencies; the Farm Security Administration gave rehabilitation loans. The Agricultural Adjustment Act controlled

134

farm production so that prices need not be depressed because of over-supply; it provided soil bank payments and commodity loans on grain in sealed storage. Farmers at first objected to the Triple-A because of Henry Wallace's pig-killing, when the government bought and slaughtered almost a half-million pigs and pregnant sows in Nebraska to keep prices up; they did not object as badly, though, when the government bought cattle to ship to market but ended up slaughtering large numbers of the poor ribby creatures who were too weak to leave the dried-up pasture. Controls on livestock production did not last long, though.

The third need was to conserve the land itself and other natural resources. The Federal Soil Conservation Act took over some of the functions of the old Triple-A, and through state conservation districts stimulated conservation, flood control practices by direct payments to farmers. Other conservation practices of the 1930's included the planting of shelter-belts and encouraging of contour planting and crop-rotation which had been advocated for years but not widely practiced.

The fourth need was to provide a retirement fund so that the specter of the Poor Farm need not haunt people nearing retirement age. That was the Social Security Act, passed in the closing days of the 1930's.

When the people of Nebraska, and the rest of the country, were plunged into the Depression, little did they realize that before they came out of it, they would have a new vocabulary and a new knowledge of the alphabet.

135

WORKING ON A PROJECTILE AT THE HASTINGS NAVAL AMMUNITION DEPOT

World War II

The bombs that burst on far-away Pearl Harbor that Sunday in December, 1941, signaled not only the beginning of another war for the United States but a new way of living for all Americans, especially for Nebraskans struggling out of a ten-year period of depression, drought and dust.

This war seemed to come with sudden drama although the country had been preparing for national defense for months. Some of the young men who had been required to register under the new Selective Service Act on October 16, 1940, had already been drafted for military training; and Nebraska's National Guard, the 134th Infantry Regiment, had been called to active duty in December, 1940. Manufacturing plants throughout the state had defense contracts or were trying to figure out how to get them. Even so, the news of an attack on America brought an emotional response. Young men hustled off to enlist; by war's end, more than 120,000 Nebraskans had served in the armed forces; of them, 3,839 lost their lives.

Nebraskans reacted to the war itself in ways they had not during World War I. Although the enemy was Germany again, there was little of the paranoia and suspicion of German-Americans that had been rampant before; there were no self-appointed super-patriots this time to harass or bully persons of German heritage. So few Japanese lived in the state that the governmental policy of relocating them meant little to Nebraskans personally.

To an area only slowly recovering from the decade of the Depression and the Dust Bowl, the war brought boom times, for almost every town became involved in the war effort in one way or another. The Martin Bomber plant in Omaha, ordnance plants in Grand Island and Mead, the enormous Naval Ammunition Depot in Hastings needed so many workers, for construction as well as for assembly-line production, that there were not enough laborers in the state. Recruiters lined up people from as far away as Indian reservations in the north and black villages in the south to work on the line; from all over the country the defense workers came. The newcomers quickly exhausted available housing in the towns involved, then the makeshift apartments created from deserted old residences, chicken-coops, carriage-houses; the Sioux and Chippewas brought into the NAD plant at Hastings put up their own teepees on the depot grounds, and blacks were housed in specially built barracks.

Before long the Army Air Corps built training bases at Alliance, Ainsworth, Bruning, Fairmont, Grand Island, Harvard, Kearney, Lincoln, McCook, Scottsbluff and Scribner, turning inland prairies into miles of concrete runways and temporary wooden barracks. Old Fort Robinson became a training center for K-9 dogs; Doane and Hastings Colleges were aviation training sites for military cadets; and later on, Atlanta was the site of a prisoner-of-war camp. The installations brought in not only men in uniform but also thousands of civilian support personnel, adding to the numbers of war workers already in the state. When the towns were jammed to capacity, newcomers had to find housing in near-by villages, using gas from their C ration stamps to drive back-and-forth to work.

Nationwide rationing of meat, butter, coffee, canned food, gasoline, shoes and other necessities began in the fall of 1942; other consumer goods were in short supply because most manufacturing production was geared for war-goods. Civilian war-workers who only a short time before had had nothing suddenly found themselves with fat pay-checks, for many of them the biggest ones they had ever seen; some people were hard-put to find ways to spend them. Hastings and Grand Island, especially, were boom-towns, for almost overnight their populations doubled with the new war workers who had neither friends nor relatives in town nor institutions to relate to in their leisure time. To accommodate them, banks, beauty shops, movie theaters and retail establishments doubled their hours of service, grandmotherly types began baby-sitting services, and with federal funding the communities began recreational activities. Under special government programs new housing was stimulated, hundreds of four and five-room houses erected quickly, along with communities of cinder-block apartments; other areas were covered with government-supplied trailers. Housing was critical. The towns were stretched to the utmost to provide utilities for the surge of newcomers, all of them needing water and electricity.

Men in uniform were housed on the base but needed recreational facilities in town. USO's sprang up, manned often by volunteers from community clubs who sponsored dances, handed out coffee and milk and cookies, and on occasion played cards with the lonesome young men. In North Platte, the USO women furnished so many millions of cookies to soldiers on troop trains going through on the Union Pacific that the town became famous nationwide. In Hastings, the thousand or so black sailors were more than the few black families in town could entertain so the Navy sponsored parties, bringing in bus-loads of black girls from Omaha, Kansas City, Des Moines, to provide chaperoned companionship.

When the war was over, most of the transients went back to their own homes, but a number remained, replacing those transplanted Nebraskans who did not return. The new prosperity carried over into the post-war years, particularly for Nebraskans who finally had enough money to fulfill the dreams they had had since the depths of the Depression more than a decade before. They mechanized and electrified their farms, built new homes, bought new cars, stoves, refrigerators. The weather smiled, the rains came, the crops on the farms were good. The next decades in Nebraska were the years of plenty.

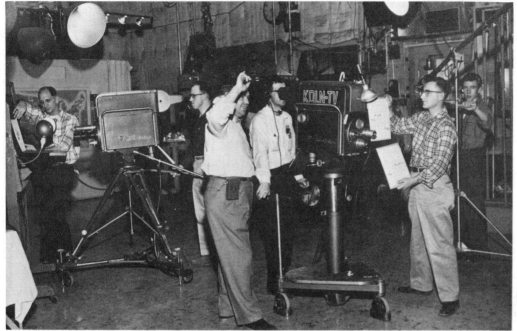

EARLY-DAY STUDIO PRODUCTION AT KOLN-TV

Television

The quiet revolution started almost without notice -- just a few box-like pieces of furniture with round or rectangular pieces of glass in them, sitting in living rooms, with grainy, jiggly pictures on the glass, the designs sometimes bouncing like a motion picture whose sprocket holes were off the track. But in 1949, when two television stations in Omaha began telecasting, the way of life for Nebraskans began to change, subtly, dramatically. Before long, the Tube would dominate their lives.

During the early 1940's, television programs were broadcast along the East Coast to the small numbers of people who had receivers, but because of the demands of World War II development of the medium did not progress. At the end of the war in 1945, however, there was an explosion of television activity, consumers eager to buy new gadgets, to find new entertainment, new excitement, and broadcasting companies, manufacturers and businessmen just as intent on providing them. When the two stations in Omaha went on the air, WOW-TV on August 29, 1949, and KMTV on September 1, 1949, Nebraskans rushed to buy television sets even though many of them were beyond reception range, even with elaborate antennas. Everyone talked about the co-axial cable which would provide coast-to-coast transmission. By 1953, when two more Nebraska stations went on the air -- KOLN-TV in Lincoln on February 18, and KHOL in Axtell on December 24 -- Nebraska waited in line for the new playthings that would open up to them the world of Jackie Gleason, Ed Sullivan, Lucy and Desi, Sid Caesar and Imogene Coco, and Groucho.

Other commercial stations began broadcasting in Nebraska: KHAS-TV in Hastings on January 1, 1956; KETV in Omaha on September 17, 1959; and KNOP in North Platte on December 15, 1958. By then television was available to a large population of the state.

In the meantime, educational television came to Nebraska, becoming in time one of the most sophisticated public television networks in the country, the nine stations and fifteen translator ones providing reception to all parts of the state. During the school year six hours of day-time telecasts provide supplemental instructional materials in classrooms, particularly useful to teachers in remote schools. Telecasts at other times of the broadcast day furnish other programs. Several originating in Lincoln have won national honors, including a 3-year series on poetry appreciation called "Anyone for Tennyson" which was presented by distinguished actors from the American and British stage. Telecasts from Lincoln are beamed from a satellite 22,000 miles above the earth, one of the five terminals for public broadcasting. When the unicameral is in session, ETV carries daily coverage from the floor of the legislature.

In January, 1976, Nebraska's ETV hit national news when NBC discovered its widely-publicized new corporate logo was the same as that which the Nebraska network had been using. In an out-of-court settlement, the ETV network agreed to let NBC have its N in return for a half-million dollars' worth of color mobile equipment; the Nebraska logo now is a lower-case n.

All Nebraska stations started out telecasting in black-and-white, changing over soon to color. In addition to the local and network shows -- three stations are NBC affiliates: KMTV, KHAS and KNOP; two are CBS: KOLN and WOWT; and two are ABC: KETV and KHGI, the new call letters from KHOL -- subscribers in a number of Nebraska communities are connected to cable-television which brings in a wide range of channels.

In the first burst of enthusiasm about television in the mid-1950's, when Nebraskans and others were glued to their tubes, watching in wonder anything that wiggled on the screen, community activities suffered. Nobody wanted to leave the easy-chair in the living room to go to concerts, plays, even movies or town-hall meetings, lest they miss "The $64,000 Question" or "Wagon Train" or some other earthshaking event on the screen at home. Now, however, community leaders have learned to schedule their meetings not to conflict with prime time telecasts and television watchers have learned that some programs they can catch on re-runs anyhow. Their vocabularies have been enlarged; re-runs and prime time, for instance, are words unfamiliar to earlier generations!

Nebraskans have contributed performers to television. Johnny Carson is the most obvious one, of course; others include Dick Cavett, the late David Janssen of "Harry O" and "The Fugitive," David Doyle of "Charlie's Angels," and James Colburn, among others. A number of other performers from Nebraska have appeared in movies which have been telecast, reaching audiences far greater than they would have in theaters. These include Marlon Brando, Henry, Jane and Peter Fonda, Dorothy McGuire, and Sandy Dennis.

Television has become big business, for Nebraskans and others select their household products, appliances and cars, seeds and fertilizers, from the suggestions bombarded to them from the screen. And the teaching of television techniques, whether in the electronics of engineering, or in the selling or producing of commercials, or in the repair of the television sets themselves, is now part of the curriculum of post-secondary schools.

In a quarter-century, television has completely revolutionized a civilization, providing instant information to millions of people so that the family in the living room can see man's first step on the moon as easily as it can a Hollywood square. Of the 578,600 households in Nebraska in 1980, a total of 566,700 have television sets, 98 per cent of the population.

J.E. MILLER AND THE MILLER & PAINE STORE AT THE CORNER OF 13TH & O,
FIRST OCCUPIED IN 1898

Happy Birthday, Miller and Paine

Happy one hundredth, Miller and Paine. You and Lincoln and Nebraska have grown up together, weathering childhood ills, adolescent traumas, and growing pains of various kinds. Now in your maturity, the store, the town, and the state are healthy and vigorous.

On the surface, none of you bear much resemblance to the youngsters you were a century ago. The Lincoln of 1980 has wide streets that are paved and clean, not rutted, dusty, and covered with litter as they were in 1880. The buildings are substantial and permanent, not hastily-thrown together wooden structures. And the state -- the fifty stories that have appeared on these pages during your anniversary year have suggested some of the changes that have taken place in Nebraska over the past century.

But what about you, Miller and Paine?

In 1880, the store was a tiny one, 22x60 feet, located at P between Tenth and Eleventh, with a closet in an adjoining building to store salt and sugar. The staple groceries, dry goods, boots and shoes that comprised the stock were traded with farmers for the butter and eggs they brought in from the country, and sold to

142

bustled and hoop-skirted townswomen who came in to buy corduroy and flannel and butter and eggs from you. Apparently all of them were pleased with the goods and services they received, for your customers followed the store as you moved to several other locations, each one a little larger than the last, until finally in 1894 you moved to a building in your present location at 13th and O.

The store itself was started in 1877 by Captain J.W. Winger and his brother-in-law James Irwin, who had moved to Lincoln three years earlier from Pennsylvania. A year later Irwin left the store, eventually going to Quincy, Illinois, where he started a printing business. Needing help in the store, Captain Winger sent back to Pennsylvania for the young man who had worked in his country store in Clay Lick, near Carlisle. John E. Miller, not yet twenty-two years old, was eager to go Out West and arrived in the capital city in the spring of 1879 to work as bookkeeper, clerk, janitor and porter. The next year the two became partners and for the next three years the store was known as Winger and Miller.

In 1883, young Miller bought out Winger's interests and set out to conduct the business himself. A legend, perhaps apocryphal, has it that young J.E. worked such long hours that his diligence came to the attention of Dr. B.L. Paine, a homeopathic physician who had come to Lincoln in 1878 from Ohio. The doctor commented that he had noticed the merchant huddled over his account books night-after-night, and suggested that he would be glad to buy in as a partner so that young Miller could hire a bookkeeper to help him in his chores. How ever the association came about, since 1889 the firm has been known as Miller and Paine, although Dr. Paine was never active in the business and the Miller family bought out his interest after his death. The store is really the work of J.E. Miller and family.

Thin, wirey, ambitious, J.E. Miller was typical in many ways of the businessmen who came to raw, new frontier communities possessed of little more than their own physical strength, desire to succeed, and ability to work long hours and handle the public. In common with most of his contemporaries, J.E. had finished school at the eighth grade, but throughout his life he read constantly so that he was a self-educated man, knowledgeable about history, philosophy, the arts, as well as business. His wife, Grace Edna Walters, whom he married in 1883 in Harrisburg, Pennsylvania, was a teacher who helped guide his early reading. In his business dealings he reflected the Puritanical attitudes of his Pennsylvania Anglo-Saxon background, for he was a man of integrity and industry. In later years he attributed his success to the ability to work hard and not being afraid of long hours; to saving money; and to being fair in his dealings, having one price for all and being truthful in advertising, understating rather than exaggerating his goods. He was never content with anything less than his best efforts, no matter the task at hand.

During the panic of 1893, when his competitors were afraid to cut prices, he did, and restocked his shelves. During the bank panics of 1903 and 1907 when others were afraid of banks, he was able to borrow large sums from them. He could sense changes in business climates before they happened; in 1887, when he switched from a general merchandise store to one which specialized in dry goods and carpets, other merchants thought him foolhardy, but he survived and they did not; he was able to glimpse the department store of the future.

Miller also believed in his town, both because a thriving community meant better business opportunities for his store but even more so because he felt a commitment to it personally. He was active in the Chamber of Commerce, the YMCA, the Lincoln General Hospital Board, on the board of St. Paul's Methodist Church, and in assorted other community functions, served as mayor for two terms beginning in 1908, and was on the University of Nebraska board of regents from 1914 to 1920. While he was a university regent, he ordered the University of Nebraska account with Miller and Paine closed so there could be no suggestion of business influence.

Miller accomplished his efforts quietly, without fanfare, but they were recognized by others. In 1924 he was awarded the Kiwanis Club medal for distinguished public service, and in 1925 an honorary Master of Arts degree from the University of Nebraska.

After J.E. Miller's death on March 15, 1938, at the age of 81, his son, D.W. Miller, became president of the company. Donald Miller was killed in an airplane accident the next year, and J.E.'s son-in-law, R.E. Campbell, became president, serving for fourteen years. In 1939, while the state was still reeling from the effects of the Depression, Miller and Paine reconstructed almost a whole block on O street by erecting an eight-story addition to the west, and building a five-story structure farther west for Ben Simon. After World War II, in 1950, Miller and Paine built the structure diagonally across the street for J.C. Penney, and with another firm, built the car-park at 13th and M, all of these investments for the business community as a whole, not for the store itself. R.E. Campbell also served as mayor of Lincoln.

Many of R.E. Campbell's contributions were innovative, ranging from the installation of the first escalators in Nebraska to forming a mutual hospital association for employees and instigating other benefits for Miller and Paine workers. He sponsored art exhibitions for young artists, used the store auditorium for international displays.

In 1953, R.E. Campbell stepped down as president to be succeeded by his son, Brigadier General John Miller Campbell, newly-released from active duty in the Air Force. A graduate in business administration from the University of Nebraska, John M. Campbell had served overseas for eighteen months in World War II, participated in seven major battles, and had been on active duty for twenty-one months during the Korean War; in fact, he received the Air Force Distinguished Service Medal on April 26, 1976, for his military contributions.

The merchandising world he stepped into was considerably different from those his father and grandfather faced, for Nebraskans and Americans everywhere were now on wheels, looking for drive-in-everything. Under John M. Campbell's direction, Miller and Paine expanded to shopping center locations. In May, 1964, the second store was opened at the Gateway Shopping Center in Lincoln, and ten years later, in February, 1974, a third one at the Conestoga Mall in Grand Island. But to encourage a return to downtown Lincoln and a revitalization of that area, John M. was a prime mover in the development of the Centrum and Skywalks, projects which opened in October, 1979, connecting two and a half blocks of retail stores in downtown Lincoln.

He has inaugurated a number of innovations within department store management, including a program wherein customers can serve as advisors through the Women's Day panels; and computerization of inventory and purchase order systems. The store was the first in the country to have completely automatic systems to read price-tags.

Standing in the wings, ready to take over when his turn comes, is 38-year-old Robert E. Campbell II, son of John M. Campbell, great-grandson of the founder of the company. He is now serving as executive vice-president and is in charge of merchandising management. Another member of the fourth generation, Carl B. Campbell, the youngest son, aged 16, is employed part-time in the store.

Author's Note

More than a year ago, when John M. Campbell first talked with me about writing this series of stories, he said he wanted material which would tell the story of Nebraska, its developments, its people. He gave me complete freedom to write about any subject I wished and in any way I desired. But when I wanted the final story to be about Miller and Paine, the company, he demurred, claiming that that would be self-serving. I have insisted, however, for I believe that Miller and Paine is a Nebraska institution which is at the same time both typical and unique, and that in this story, readers can absorb additional Nebraska history. The company is typical in that it is similar to many other small, closely-held family businesses started a century ago by eager, hard-working young entrepreneurs from the East. But it is unique in that it has survived, growing in size and importance while remaining a family-held institution with its original business philosophy. From this story, I believe readers can detect some of the qualities that have given Nebraska its strength and vigor.

Other Books about Nebraska

If you are interested in reading more about the history of Nebraska, you have a wide range of books to choose from. In addition to a number of general histories in print, there are scores of other volumes which tell the stories of towns or villages or counties.

General Histories

Dorothy Weyer Creigh, *Nebraska: A Bicentennial History,* W.W. Norton, 1977, is the source of the material in some of the stories in this book. The volume focuses particularly on the people, who they were, where they came from, and their relationship to the land.

Virginia Faulkner, Editor, *A Nebraska Reader,* University of Nebraska Press, 1957, contains provocative essays by a number of writers on many topics about Nebraska. This volume is not a history as such, but contains superb writing about our favorite state.

James C. Olson, *Nebraska,* 1955 reprinted University of Nebraska Press, 1966, is a balanced history of the state, outlining political developments as well as economic ones. This is the standard text on the history of Nebraska, and is a great one.

Mari Sandoz, *Love Song to the Plains,* 1961, reprinted University of Nebraska Press, 1966, is based somewhat on Olson's book, focuses more on western Nebraska than on the state as a whole. It also contains tall tales and details about Indians not found in other books.

Walter Prescott Webb, *The Great Plains,* 1931, reprinted Grosset and Dunlap, 1972, is not a history of Nebraska as such but tells about Nebraska's place in the Great Plains.

Older Histories

Who's Who in Nebraska, (Nebraska Press Association, 1940), contains brief county histories written by local newspaper editors. The accuracy and balance of the accounts vary, depending on the scholarship and objectivity of the authors.

Addison E. Sheldon, *Nebraska: The Land and the People,* (Lewis Publishing Company, 1931) is a 3-volume work, the first volume being a detailed political history of the state. He does have his prejudices -- who doesn't -- but you can quickly discern them as you read, and can make allowances for them.

J. Sterling Morton and Albert Watkins, *Illustrated History of Nebraska,* (Jacob North and Company, 1907, 1912), is another 3-volume work, most of the history contained in the first volume. Probably the best of the early histories.

A.T. Andreas, *History of Nebraska,* 1882, reprinted in two volumes by the Nebraska State Historical Society, 1976. Since the county chapters were written by individual local newspaper editors, the quality of research and writing varies widely. Some of the material is far-fetched, some of it puffery, but it's fascinating reading nevertheless.

Biographical and Historical Memoirs of various counties, published by the Goodspeed Publishing Company in the 1890's and early 1900's, and various county histories published by the S.J. Clarke Company between 1910 and 1920. Goodspeed relies heavily on Andreas, therefore compounding the errors therein; the Clarke volumes were usually written by local newspaper editors and their quality varies.

Local and County Histories

Almost every county in the state has had some histories written, some of them recent vintage, others from long ago. Consult your local historical society or the Nebraska State Historical Society librarian. Some are hard-cover volumes, others paperback; some are excellent, some woefully inadequate. But each one has information of interest to people who are interested in the history of their own particular localities.

Other Books

Nebraskans have an enviable source of material about Nebraska history through the Bison paperback books published by the University of Nebraska Press, reprints of books published earlier. Most libraries and all bookshops have catalogs of Bison books in print. They range from Andy Adam's *Log of a Cowboy,* telling about the cattle trail and Ogallala, to *Nebraska: A Guide to the Cornhusker State,* a reprint of the 1939 WPA directory, and cover a wide range of topics.

A few specific other books are mentioned in the stories in this volume.

Index

Acknowledgements

Few writer-historians have ever been given such a blank-check as I was when John M. Campbell, president of Miller and Paine, suggested that for the centennial celebration of his company I write a series of stories about Nebraska for a newspaper audience. He gave me complete freedom as to subject matter, format and style of presentation, number of stories and length. The series was a magnificent opportunity to present to a wide public short readable stories which tell about the people in the state and how they have lived.

To John M. Campbell, then, my thanks for this opportunity.

To Anne Reinert, librarian of the Nebraska State Historical Society, my great appreciation for her hours and hours of research to locate much of the historical data which these stories required. She answered my urgent phone calls, my letters, with dispatch, performing far beyond the call of duty.

To John Carter, photo librarian of the Nebraska State Historical Society, who worked with Alice Pederson of the Miller and Paine art staff in suggesting and locating appropriate photographs to illustrate the stories. His intimate knowledge of the vast photographic holdings of the society was invaluable.

To Alice Pederson, who performed the chore each week of reducing manuscripts to readable newspaper copy, manipulating pictures to fit the somewhat erratic lengths of the stories; who designed the distinctive border for the newspaper stories; who did the watercolor painting for the cover; and who spent tedious hours designing the book itself and supervising the details.

To Doc Chaves of the Miller and Paine staff who acted as go-between for the author and the M&P art staff, cheerfully attending to even the most trivial of questions.

To Warren Joyce Ayres, who was in on the project from the beginning; who handled all the negotiations with the printer.

To Thelma Sole of the Hastings Public Library, who cheerfully rassled with the dozens of inter-library loan books I requested of her for data on specific subjects.

To James Ackerman, for faithfully mailing copies each week; to Lois Weyand, for clipping, laminating and mailing others.

To Milt Klint, Walter Thompson, A. James Ebel, Duane Watts, Toni Weiler, Thom Snell, Rosalie Fuller, Joe Di Natale, J.L. Scroggins, James T. Hansen, Charles C. Osborne, Ben Rogge, Norma Hoffman, Jasper D. Skinner, and dozens of others from whom I sought and found specific information for specific stories.

To the scores of readers who sent letters or otherwise communicated to offer their thanks, their suggestions, even their approval of the stories.

To my father, Dean F.E. Weyer, for his intimate knowledge of Nebraska history gained from his ninety years of vigorous living.

To my husband, Thomas Creigh, Jr., who suggested the title of this book after an ad hoc committee had agonized for weeks over it, and who offered in his usual quiet unflappable way the support I needed for the hours of intensive labor.

To my three sons, Tom, John and Jaimie, who understood why Mommy needed peace and quiet while she was huddled over the typewriter.

DOROTHY WEYER CREIGH

Hastings
1 October 1980